Family-Focused
Trauma Intervention

Family-Focused Trauma Intervention

Using Metaphor and Play with Victims of Abuse and Neglect

Pat Pernicano, PsyD

JASON ARONSON

Lanham • Boulder • New York • Toronto • Plymouth, UK

Published by Jason Aronson
An imprint of Rowman & Littlefield Publishers, Inc.
A wholly owned subsidary of The Rowman & Littlefield Publishing Group, Inc.
4501 Forbes Boulevard, Suite 200, Lanham, Maryland 20706
http://www.rowmanlittlefield.com

Estover Road, Plymouth PL6 7PY, United Kingdom

British Library Cataloguing in Publication Information Available

Library of Congress Cataloging-in-Publication Data
Pernicano, Pat, 1954–
  Family-focused trauma intervention : using metaphor and play with victims of
abuse and neglect / Pat Pernicano.
     p.   cm.
  Includes bibliographical references and index.
  ISBN 978-0-7657-0772-7 (cloth : alk. paper) — ISBN 978-0-7657-0774-1
(electronic)
  1. Psychic trauma in children. 2. Abused children—Psychology. 3. Abused
children—Rehabilitation. 4. Child psychotherapy. 5. Family psychotherapy. I.
Title.
  RJ506.P66P47 2010
  618.92'8521—dc22

                                                          2009050674

∞ ™ The paper used in this publication meets the minimum requirements of
American National Standard for Information Sciences—Permanence of Paper
for Printed Library Materials, ANSI/NISO Z39.48-1992.

Printed in the United States of America

Contents

Acknowledgments

I dedicate this volume to the clients at Seven Counties Services and Providence House for Children who inspired these stories.

I would like to recognize Spalding doctoral students Lily Cooksey, Valerie Fallon, Laura Gabel, Candice Holmes, Meg Hornsby, and Jody Pimentel for their creativity and loving commitment to the children and families at Providence House for Children.

I owe special thanks to my son, Sam, for being my #1 fan and reviewer of many of the stories and to my daughter, Becky, for believing in me. Finally, I am grateful to my loving husband, Kevin, who provided hours of tireless proofreading and endless encouragement.

Introduction

Families that have experienced abuse, neglect, and/or domestic violence benefit from specialized, family-focused interventions that help them build new coping skills and remediate the effects of trauma. This book provides metaphorical stories and interventions (play, experiential, and cognitive-behavioral) that facilitate the healing process and help children and their families understand the effects of trauma.

The book is primarily a selection of trauma and recovery-focused metaphorical stories that "springboard" children and families into discussing, with less avoidance, traumatic experiences and how they have been affected by them. There are also a number of stories focused on coping skills and the change process. The stories and subsequent interventions help children and their parents make meaning of life events, reduce arousal, increase self-efficacy, and bolster trust and attachment.

Effective trauma interventions may be packaged and delivered in many different ways, as long as they access emotion, tap into neurological pathways affected by trauma, decrease arousal, build coping skills, and change perception. We recommend an integrative therapy model that is family-focused and attachment-driven. Throughout these chapters, the reader is likely to recognize concepts from Gil and Briere (2006), Cohen et al.'s (2004) trauma-focused cognitive behavioral therapy (TF-CBT), and the ARC model proposed by Bessel van der Kolk and his colleagues as found on the Trauma Center website (www.traumacenter.org/research/ascot.php).

Cohen et al.'s TF-CBT is currently the gold standard of PTSD treatment for children—an excellent, comprehensive program—but after program completion, 10–15 percent of children still meet criteria for PTSD, and multiply-traumatized children are difficult to treat (Mannarino 2009). The interventions and stories in this book may be used in conjunction with TF-CBT, particularly with children who are multiply traumatized and require longer-term intervention due to avoidance, heightened affect, and problematic behavior. The issues addressed in this book are similar to those contained within the ARC model of trauma intervention.

Many books about using therapeutic metaphor to treat children and adults have been published in recent years (Burns 2005, 2007; Kaduson & Schaefer 2003; and Kopp 1995). These books skillfully lay out techniques and interventions for the use of metaphors, and the Burns edited volume (2007) includes examples of the ways in which well-established practitioners have used therapeutic metaphor in their own work.

Metaphor and storytelling have been used within a variety of conceptual orientations: solution oriented (O'Hanlon & Martin 1992), Ericksonian hypnosis (Brown 1991; Gafner & Benson 2003), child hypnotherapy (Olness & Kohen 1996), narrative therapy (Smith & Nylund 1997), mindfulness (Hayes et al. 2004), body-mind psychotherapy (Levine & Frederick 1997), and cognitive behavioral play therapies (Drewes 2009). Depending on the orientation, metaphor and storytelling may be considered techniques to "seed" change, cognitive behavioral scripts, a hypnotic intervention somewhat nonconscious in nature, utilization of the client's presenting issues for insight, narrative to help a client see things differently, an "aha moment," a teaching technique, or a means of reducing defensive and resistance. In *101 Healing Stories for Kids and Teens* (2005), Burns indicates that stories inform, educate, teach values, discipline, build experience, facilitate problem solving, and change/heal.

This author views metaphor similarly to Burns (2007), who describes it as a special, expressive form of communication. Henry Close (1998) points out that metaphor allows therapists and clients to "bypass power struggles." It is a tool, the foundation of descriptive literature that depicts different perspectives on real situations. Metaphor invites identification and is more believable and memorable than other therapeutic "teaching" techniques. The characters can even be matched to the story's themes. For example, a basset hound nicely depicts a depressed client, more nicely than, say, would a French poodle. An alligator is more malevolent than a cute kangaroo, and a fire-breathing dragon is an easy metaphor for anger.

Metaphorical stories are interactive, and they hold interest, engage imagination, and "sneak through" the back door so as to eliminate resistance. They stimulate a personal "search" for meaning and facilitate problem-solving skills. Metaphors offer possibility, but it is the client who selects the outcome.

Metaphorical stories capture interest for a number of reasons and in a number of ways. For example, the characters and their thoughts, feelings, or behaviors may "match" the client's. While listening to a story that has been selected by the therapist, the client may *recognize* his or her similarity to a character in the story. A client may or may not yet have recognized aspects of a problem or how to solve it. The story's themes may open up other ways to look at things.

Regardless of theoretical orientation, there seem to be common ways in which metaphors are used in therapy:

1. Therapist conceptualizes the client's core issues and barriers to dealing with those issues.
2. Therapist may select a story in which one or more characters have characteristics similar to the client's (thoughts, feelings, or coping style).
3. Therapist may use a metaphor or story to interpret something shared by the client—therapist utilizes a metaphor used by the client in session or creates one.
4. Therapist may select and share a metaphor or story that matches the client's core concerns or core barriers.
5. Therapist may select and share a metaphor or story that includes characters similar to those in client's life or past life.
6. Therapist may select and share a metaphor or story that uses evidence-based interventions relevant to the client's issues.
7. Therapist may select and share a metaphor or story that suggests possible solutions not yet realized by the client.

The use of metaphorical stories in treatment may be planned or unplanned. When doing a parenting group, I often go in with a story in mind. But other times, the use of a story is spontaneous, elicited by the process of the client. It is always the case that stories springboard clients into discussion and many will express feelings of being understood or identify the similarity between themselves and one or more of the story's characters.

Once the therapist becomes familiar with a good selection of metaphorical stories and their characters, the stories will come to mind as clients share their experiences. Generally, I hear something that reminds me of a particular story or character, then offer to share a story with the client, family, or group of clients. It is the client's response to the story that determines the next step of treatment.

This volume is a unique collection of metaphorical stories and interventions designed for specialized work in trauma recovery; the stories may be used again and again with those clients for whom they are a "good fit." The themes and metaphors in the stories are particularly relevant to those who have experienced abuse or neglect.

When abuse or neglect is substantiated on someone in the home, the goal for treatment may be family reunification, termination of parental rights, or out-of-home placement. For family reunification, family relationships ultimately need to change, not just the individuals within the family. Even when the abuse is by someone outside the family, the parent-child relationships must be addressed in terms of safety and protection. Programs for family violence rarely treat the family as a unit, and few programs address the cross-generational trauma that is often present in CPS-involved families. When community programs focus exclusively on education and skills development, individuals learn to say what professionals "want to hear" and to do what is expected of them in order to get through the court system; the process becomes one more of compliance than of change.

Additionally, programs that are "top down" and confrontational impede client "buy-in" and do not usually ignite motivation to change. Sometimes, even after weeks or months of typical outpatient services, client change is "only skin deep." I was explaining the *desired*, relational change process to a friend of mine, who is an Avon consultant. She said, "It's like the difference between *moisturizing the skin on the surface* with skin moisturizer and *changing the chemical structure of the skin underneath* using skin treatment." There is a need for family-focused trauma interventions that change the "chemical structure" of the relationships among family members and interventions that will ultimately lead to neurobiological stabilization.

To develop nurturing and protective relationships with their children, parents need to see the past for what it was, take responsibility for their own behavior, develop empathy and attachment, put their children's needs before their own, and become trustworthy adults. As part of the change process, they must resolve their own family-of-origin issues. Inside each abusive/neglectful parent lives a child or teen still acting out his or her own disrupted attachment.

Children in abusive or neglectful families need to decrease arousal, resolve hurt and loss, feel safe in the present (and know what to do if things become unsafe), develop new and realistic trust, and learn how to be children again. They benefit from integrative therapies (play-based, experiential, interpersonal, and cognitive behavioral) that teach coping skills and calm physiological arousal by altering neurological pathways that were damaged as a result of trauma.

The change process described above is a difficult one. According to Jeff Zeig (2008) during a workshop in Louisville, Kentucky, if a treatment provider "connects the dots *for*" clients and does not encourage them to "come up with" their own solutions, clients do little more than follow the left brain dotted line of compliance. The therapist must guide the *family* to connect the dots of their own lives in an emotionally meaningful way.

The stories and techniques in this manuscript arose out of my clinical work at Providence House for Children, a group home and family preservation program for abused and neglected children and their families in Georgetown, Indiana, and at Seven Counties Services, a community mental health center in Louisville, Kentucky. The cases have been de-identified to protect client confidentiality.

Each chapter in this book addresses a central theme in trauma recovery. The stories and therapy activities facilitate the change process and allow families to connect the dots of their family history in a new way. As a result, therapists will be able to propel change that is more than skin deep.

1

Impact of Trauma and Overview of Treatment

Neurological and biological changes, observable with neuro-imaging techniques, occur as a result of abuse or exposure to abuse (McCollum 2006). These changes contribute to medical, social, behavioral, and emotional problems during childhood and later in life.

McCollum (2006) nicely summarizes research regarding the effects of trauma on brain development. The limbic system, which initiates, controls, and inhibits emotions, is the part of the brain most vulnerable to adverse childhood experiences. McCollum indicates that those with trauma reactions show altered cognitive and affective processing, as well as limbic and motor activation in response to trauma triggers. The limbic system links emotional reactions with physical responses and is involved in evaluation of and response to perceived danger and interpreting facial expressions. The "fight or flight" response to stress largely arises within the limbic system; and components of the limbic system are involved in memory and learning. Trauma also "primes" individuals to over-react to subsequent stressors, making them more vulnerable to such events.

Children raised in violent, abusive, or neglectful homes may display (as children or later as adults) violent or angry behavior, sexual reactivity or aggression, insecure attachment, symptoms of anxiety and depression, ADHD symptoms, excitability, dissociation, hallucinations, and substance abuse (McCollum 2006). It was once assumed that social learning (modeling, imitation, and reinforcement) accounted for most symptoms of PTSD; but some of the symptoms that follow abuse are related to physiological and neurological changes mentioned above.

McCollum (2006) also summarizes research about health problems that may be linked to childhood maltreatment: chronic fatigue syndrome, fibromyalgia, auto-immune disorders such as lupus, pre-term labor, chronic pain syndromes, and ovarian dysfunction. Repeated childhood trauma may result in chronic elevation of stress hormones, reduce the size of some brain structures, and increase the size of ventricles. Dopamine levels increase in response to chronic stress, and increased dopamine can lead to paranoid/ psychotic behavior, reduced attention, increased vigilance, and difficulty learning new material. Serotonin levels decrease in response to chronic stress; and low serotonin levels have been linked to suicidal behavior, depression, and aggression.

Treatments vary depending on age and source of trauma, but they must be integrative, holistic, and multi-modal to address the array of symptoms. There are a variety of evidence-based and effective practices to treat PTSD.

Trauma-focused cognitive behavioral therapy, known as TF-CBT (Cohen et al. 2004), is a comprehensive program that involves parents and children in parallel activities with components such as stress management, mood modulation, attachment, safety, personal narrative, and relaxation.

Gil and Briere (2006) propose an integrated model of developmentally appropriate treatment for traumatized children. Cohen et al. (2004) provide a variety of easily individualized expressive, play, and family therapy interventions. Cognitive behavioral and play therapies may be combined for use with young children and their families (Drewes 2009). For very young or developmentally delayed children, trauma memories may be non-cognitive, embedded in right brain areas, with sensory and neurological components. Such memories are more easily accessed and treated through play and expressive modalities, especially since, for young children, play is the primary mode of communication.

At the Evolution of Psychotherapy Conference in Anaheim, California, in 2004, Dr. Bessel van der Kolk presented research on PTSD using brain-imaging data. Dr. van der Kolk indicated that when individuals used verbal means to "tell" their stories, left brain areas were very active, while right brain, emotional centers would shut down. Conversely, when individuals were experiencing strong affect associated with traumatic events, the right brain emotional areas were very active, often flooding them with arousal, while the left brain verbal narrative areas were shut down. It was Dr. van der Kolk's view that integrative therapies, including "body-mind" type therapies, would allow individuals to more effectively resolve trauma symptoms.

There is promising support for the use of less traditional "body-mind" type therapies, such as hypnosis, EMDR, acupuncture, yoga, meditation, guided imagery, and therapeutic massage. Such therapies appear to lead to changes in the arousal and trauma response mechanisms (Kinniburgh et al. 2005). At the Trauma Center, Dr. Bessel van der Kolk and his colleagues have been conducting an outcome trial on attachment, self-regulation, and competency, otherwise known as ARC (Kinniburgh et al. 2005). ARC is a model for treatment of trauma victims—it is not a set of techniques nor a manual approach but one that identifies core issues for treatment. ARC is a comprehensive framework for intervention, tailored to each client's needs, and may include individual and group therapy for children, education for caregivers, parent-child sessions, and parent workshops.

At www.traumacenter.org/research/ascot.php, a thorough description of ARC and the ARC study is available. ARC is utilized with youth and families who have experienced multiple and/or prolonged traumatic stress. ARC identifies three core domains necessary for resiliency—ones impacted by trauma in children and families.

The three domains needed for healthy functioning are attachment, self-regulation, and competency (Kinniburgh & Blaustein 2005). The focus of the attachment work is on caregiver, consistent response, attunement, and family routines and rituals. Self-regulation addresses affect management, affect identification, affect modulation, and affect expression. They target self-efficacy, developmental tasks, executive functioning, and self-development to build competency.

Preliminary data from pilot studies indicate that ARC leads to reduction in child posttraumatic stress symptoms, anxiety, and depression, as well as increased adaptive and social skills. Caregivers report reduced distress and view their children's behaviors as less dysfunctional. ARC principles have successfully been applied in a range of settings, including outpatient clinics, residential treatment centers, schools, and day programs.

The above research supports this author's view that treatment must be integrative, including components to decrease physiological arousal as well as components for cognitive restructuring. Within families, it is important to alter relational and environmental factors that trigger arousal. Without early intervention, the long-term ramifications of abuse and neglect are significant.

The stories and interventions that follow in this chapter, useful in individual, family, or group therapy, are recommended for use in early and middle phase treatment, to educate clients about the effects of trauma.

PTSD

The first story in this section, *A Bear of a Different Color*, is a powerful metaphor for the experience of trauma. Adults and children alike have related to Bear feeling tarnished "outside and in" and to springboard into discussion of their own trauma events. A nine-year-old victim of repeated abuse created the bear and the pit during an expressive therapy activity. Using a dry erase board, she and the author played the "squiggles story" game (see appendix).

She drew a long tangled pathway, a large black pit, a red platform in the pit, two guards in front of the pit, red things floating in the pit, and a frantic-looking black bear.

The client was asked to tell a story about her picture. She said that the black bear (who used to be brown) got past the guards, fell in the pit, and turned black from stuff in the bottom of the pit. The bear survived the fall by landing on a red trampoline but broke its back. She announced that if someone were to fall in and land behind the trampoline, he or she would die. The floating red things were the hearts of those that died.

She and her brothers had been physically and sexually abused in three consecutive homes over a period of eight years. All three had significant trauma symptoms and did not respond to conventional trauma-based treatment. This author wrote the story *A Bear of a Different Color* and read it to the little girl as a lead-in to her talking about and processing her trauma experiences, something she had been avoiding. She grew anxious as the story was read, rocking furiously, but she remained intensely focused. At the point where the bear was rescued, she exclaimed, "That's *my* story! Don't leave him black! You have to clean him up!" The therapist reassured her that we would help the bear get "cleaned up" and finished reading the story.

After hearing the story, this young client moved immediately (later that day) with her therapist into intense, focused trauma work. To that point, she had avoided direct discussion of her own abuse, and much of her anxiety had been channeled into compulsive behaviors.

It is helpful to utilize this story early in treatment to focus on the experience and effects of trauma on the individual. Later on, the same story may be used with a body-tracing activity to guide the client in talking about his/her abuse/neglect, help the client lower arousal, and carry out cognitive restructuring. Abuse victims of all ages will relate to this story as they discuss their symptoms, identify their own "black areas," and share their trauma narratives.

A BEAR OF A DIFFERENT COLOR (dedicated to K)

Bear Bear, a small black bear, frowned. "I should be happy," Bear complained in a grouchy voice. "I should be happy to be out of the pit. But noooooo, I'm still not happy."

Bear's best friend, Brown Squirrel, scrambled down a nearby tree trunk and raced over to where Bear was complaining. Squirrel, with a large acorn in his mouth, asked, "Mwass wongh?"

Bear said, "Squirrel, with that acorn in your mouth, I can't understand what you're saying."

Squirrel smiled, spit out the acorn, and said, more clearly, "What's wrong?"

Bear replied, "I'm having bad dreams about falling in the black pit and I'm afraid to walk in the forest. I want my old life back—I used to be a happy, brown bear. I was born brown, and that's the way I liked it. Well, now I'm not brown and I'm not happy!"

The black pit that Bear was talking about was on the other side of the forest. You might be wondering how a little bear had happened to fall into such a pit. Well, as they say, "One thing leads to another."

It was just starting to get dark outside the afternoon Bear decided to take a walk in the forest. Bear didn't realize how late in the day it was. Then Bear found a honey tree and got a little distracted trying to get some honey out of the tree without being stung by bees.

Before Bear knew it, it was dark. In the darkness, Bear took the wrong path—the one that led to the pit.

"There are warning signs for the pit on that path," you say. "Ones that say 'Danger—do not go any further!' and 'Danger, deep black pit ahead!' Why didn't Bear see them and stop?"

Well, the pit's warning signs were too small, and Bear could not see them in the dark.

"But what about the guards?" you ask. "There are guards posted in front of the pit!"

That's true—there were two guards sitting in front of the pit, and they were supposed to stay awake and alert. But they had fallen asleep and could not warn Bear of the danger ahead.

Since Bear did not see the warning signs and the guards were asleep, you can imagine what happened. Yes, Bear fell into the deep, dark pit. When Bear hit the bottom of the pit, black, nasty, sticky, smelly goop splashed all around and covered Bear from head to toe. Bear survived the fall, but lay there for hours with a broken back.

"Please help me, somebody—anybody!" Bear cried out in pain for several long hours. Finally, a deer running through the woods heard Bear's cries and woke up the guards. That is how Bear got rescued from the pit and taken to the hospital.

The hospital fixed Bear's broken back, but no one could figure out how to wash off the black goop. The goop was an awful reminder of the fall, and Bear wanted to "come clean."

Squirrel wrinkled up his bushy brow and said, "Ah, so that's what's wrong, Bear. The fall into the pit changed you. You want to be brown again and you want to be happy. Let's go to the Recovery Center. It is a healing place. Maybe they can figure out how to help you."

It was a long walk to the Recovery Center. When they arrived, Squirrel said, "Go ahead, Bear, just knock on the front door and tell them why we're here."

Bear knocked sharply on the broad wooden door. The door opened.

"May I help you?" asked a kind voice.

"Yes," said Bear. "My name is Bear Bear, and this is my friend Squirrel. I fell in the dangerous pit on the other side of the forest—the one where the guards sit day and night. I got covered with black, smelly goop. My friend thought that you might be able to help me."

"Hello, Bear and Squirrel," said the person. "Please come inside."

Bear and Squirrel stepped through the open door to enter the Recovery Center, which smelled really nice and looked a little like a health spa. As you walked in, you could hear the sounds of ocean waves. There were colorful flowers all around and healers of all types providing hugs, refreshments, and music.

"Look, Squirrel!" said Bear in an excited voice. He pointed to a big hot tub in the middle of the room, one with purple bubbles bubbling on top. Next to the hot tub was a fountain with sweet-smelling green slime gurgling out of it. There was a pile of spa towels for when you got out of the hot tub, as soft as down blankets—and believe it or not, they even smelled like whipped cream!

Once they were inside, the person said, "I am a healer, and I know about that awful pit. Many children fall in when the guards are asleep. It is a terrible thing indeed. Sometimes, children are at the pit's edge before they realize where they are, and then it is too late. It's a good thing you survived, because many do not."

Bear told the healer, "I'm glad I survived, but I want to be brown again, more than anything else in the world."

The healer replied, "I can help you get rid of the black goop, but it's not an easy cure."

"Does the cure hurt?" asked Bear.

The healer answered, "Yes, but it is not as painful as falling in the pit. The healing takes a little time, so you can't be in a hurry. But I am a gentle healer, and I'll help you if that is what you want."

"Yes," said Bear and Squirrel at the same time. "Please help!"

The healer said, "To wash off the black goop, you must soak in the hot tub." So Bear stepped down into the hot tub with all the purple bubbles. It was very hot and burned Bear's sensitive skin, enough to make the little bear cry.

"I'm sorry, little bear," said the healer. "I know that the healing waters hurt at first."

Bear sat in the tub, and Squirrel sat right there next to Bear, offering his paw to hold. Bear said, "Thank you, Squirrel. I'm glad I don't have to go through this alone!"

"It's OK, Bear," said Squirrel. "You're worth it!"

The hot solution bubbled around Bear and soaked all the way deep down through the black goop into Bear's skin. Little by little, it washed Bear clean. Then the healer helped Bear out of the tub, offered a soft towel, and provided a nice-smelling lotion for Bear's tender skin. Bear was now a lovely golden brown color.

"Can I look in a mirror?" asked Bear. The healer led Bear to a mirror. Bear stood still for a few minutes, looked in the mirror, and said, "I can see that the black goop is gone and I'm brown again. But I still don't feel happy. I don't want to complain, but the hot tub didn't fix that."

The healer said, "When you fell in the pit, you were so shocked and scared that you gulped in some of the black goop. Getting rid of the black goop on the outside doesn't get rid of the black goop on the inside."

"Inside me?" asked Bear with horror. "How can I get rid of something bad inside me that I can't even see?"

"You need to go through a second type of healing," the healer said.

"I'll do whatever you say," said Bear.

The healer told Bear, "For the second type of healing, you pick out a special healing potion and drink it. After you drink the potion, you tell your story. That's what makes the potion work."

"My story?" asked Bear.

"You know," said the healer. "The story of how you fell in the pit and what happened to you—how awful it is that the guards didn't keep you safe, and how you felt when you realized you were falling and might die; how you landed in the black, smelly goop and broke your back; and how scared you were when you thought you would never get out of there alive."

Bear argued, "I'll drink the potion, but I won't talk about the fall or the pit. I spend almost every waking moment trying not to think about falling in the pit. Talking about it would make it even worse."

"Well," said the healer in a gentle voice, "that's the only way to heal inside. As you tell your story, the potion dissolves the black goop. Once the healing is done, you'll stop having bad dreams and stop thinking about falling in the pit."

Bear thought hard about how much better life would be if the nasty, black goop was gone, outside and in and said, "OK, I'll drink the potion and talk about what happened to me. I don't really have a choice."

"You always have a choice," said the healer.

It was true. Bear had a choice. So Bear picked a potion that was all the colors of the rainbow and swallowed it down. It was warm and tasty, and it quickly spread all through Bear's body.

After Bear drank the potion, the healer said, "When you feel ready, Bear, start at the beginning, and tell your story. It's OK to start and stop. Just get it all out, a little at a time."

So Bear told the story of Bear's fall in the pit, one memory at a time. For Bear, it was an awful reliving of fear and pain, and Bear wondered if the tears would ever stop. But Bear stuck with it, and day by day, spot by spot, the black goop inside disappeared. Bear could feel the healing taking place. The tears finally stopped, and something like relief took its place.

Then one day, Bear said to the healer, "You know, I have stopped having bad dreams about falling in the pit. I can think about that time without my heart pounding. The memory has even faded a bit. I feel much better!"

The healer replied "Congratulations! That means the black goop is pretty much gone. You have been very brave. I think your healing is complete, and it is time for you to move on. "

"Hip, hip, hooray!" shouted Squirrel and Bear at the news of Bear's success.

"By the way," added the healer, "We put a good fence around the pit and installed an alarm system for protection. There is NO WAY you or anyone else will ever fall in that pit again."

Bear hugged the healer and all the staff, thanked them for their help, and left the Recovery Center with Squirrel. As they walked away from the center, they saw the sun shining through dark rain clouds, and a large rainbow appeared in the sky.

"Maybe that rainbow is a sign," said Bear to Squirrel. "A sign that better times are ahead."

"I'm sure that's so," said Squirrel, "And you deserve it!"

"Thanks," said Bear. "I couldn't have done it without you."

THE BOTTOM LINE: Do what you need to do to heal, outside and in.

Treatment Interventions

Bear Drawing Activity

1. After reading the story to or with the client, ask him or her to draw his or her depiction of the "pit" and the "brown-to-black bear." We suggest using a dry erase board and photographing the stages of the drawing. We have found that children's dry erase drawings more clearly display trauma process. Children enjoy having control over the drawing and being able to erase mistakes or change the drawing as they go, which reinforces the concept that *change is possible in their own lives.* Therapist should get client permission to photograph stages of the drawing(s) and print them for the child. A collection of art may be easily saved as a PowerPoint file or in a folder to put into the child's storybook.
2. Discuss the client's drawing and the story with the client. Ask what made the bear turn black and how it made the bear feel.
3. Link the bear's experience to child abuse and ask what sorts of things leave "black goop" on children. Ask the child how someone feels outside and in following abuse. Ask the child if he or she has ever felt like the bear.

Bear Body-Tracing Activity

1. Body tracing: help client make a body tracing on mural paper and add identifying characteristics as well as a bright red valentine heart where the child's heart would be.
2. Tell client that perhaps he or she is like the bear in that parts were hurt by the abuse (outside and in). Suggest that hurt may have been physical, sexual, emotional (in the heart), or in the brain (thoughts).
3. Ask client to mark the body with "black goop dots" where he or she was hurt outside and in by abuse. Suggest that the child make the black areas biggest where the hurt was biggest and smaller where the hurt was less.
4. Give much positive reinforcement, and in cases where the child has left out a known hurt, ask the child, "Did anyone hurt you there?" and point to the part.
5. Tell client that as he or she talks about the abuse over the next few weeks, the child can erase black spots or cover them with whiteout/white paint, and that telling the story will help the client heal.

Bear Trauma Narrative

1. Therapist provides a "potion" that the child likes (soft drink, juice, etc.). Therapist tells child that he or she will select "black goop" areas on the body tracing, one at a time.

2. Therapist reminds the child that he or she will heal inside, like the little bear, and feel better by talking about what happened. Therapist facilitates client telling his/her story, one "black goop area" at a time.

3. Therapist asks child's permission to write down or record the child's story as he/she talks about the "black goop" areas. The child is free to pick any black area to start telling his or her story. Videotape the story or take notes.

4. Therapist may use a digital or phone camera to capture the process of the child gradually erasing the black areas. As each part of the story is told and the client indicates that he or she is finished, client "erases" the black areas on the self by painting over them with paint of a different color or with whiteout/white paint.

5. This process will take a number of sessions, as it constitutes prolonged exposure. Therapist should follow the client's lead, backing off briefly or taking a break if there are signs of numbing or avoidance.

6. Encourage the child to share his or her drawing and story with trusted others. This enhances self-efficacy.

7. If more than one person has hurt the child in the past, address one perpetrator's behavior at a time. The "black goop" areas, in that case, will be areas hurt by that particular person.

Alternate Trauma Narrative: A Night at the Movies

This technique provides some psychological distance to help the child talk about abuse and some structure for the child to better use his/her senses for detailed recall. Therapist should listen and watch for signs that the child is becoming overwhelmed and suggest the child pause and use deep breathing if that happens.

1. Therapist tells the child, "It's hard to talk about the bad things that happened to you. But it's important to remember what happened and to talk about it."

2. Therapist: "Let's pretend that what happened to you got recorded on a DVD movie. It is a DVD of the time you got (touched, hurt, abused, etc.) by X."

3. The therapist educates child that our senses help us remember things: what we saw, what we touched or what touched us, what we smelled, what we heard, what we felt, and what we tasted. Therapist gives the child the handout of Use Your Common Senses (see page 18).

4. "This worksheet might help you remember all the details and not leave anything out. Before we watch the DVD I want you to use your memory and think about each of these things. For example,

you might want to picture what you were wearing that day, where you were when it happened, who else was there, and what time of year it was."

5. Next, therapist pretends to hand the child an invisible remote that has been cut out of cardboard (see page 20 for a handout you can photocopy) and says, "This is a special remote control—you can push 'play,' 'pause,' 'stop,' or 'eject.' When you push 'play,' the DVD will start showing the time you got (touched, hurt, abused, etc.) by X. Let's put the screen over there on my wall. I'd like you tell me what happens as we watch the DVD."

6. Therapist reminds the child that the office is a safe place and that if the child gets scared or thinks he/she is back *IN* the memory, it is OK to pause to take a deep breath, stop the DVD, or "come back" to the office.

7. The therapist hands the child the invisible remote and says, "OK, you can push 'play.'"

8. Therapist pretends that an image is being projected on a wall in his/her office. "Look—over there on the screen. It's you. Do you see it?"

9. The therapist talks the child through the DVD and provides emotional support. Useful questions include, "What do you see? What do you hear? Where are you? Who else is home? Day or night? What happens next? It's OK, remember we're here in my office. What did that person say?" When the child is done, therapist praises the child for being brave.

Changing the Story

Therapists can use the handout on page 18 to help the child discuss their traumatic memories in more detail. At some point after the child has viewed and talked about the abuse, *and when there is no risk of contaminating court testimony*, therapist tells the child that they will be changing the bad memories. This exercise is an opportunity for a child to alter the outcome, meaning, or context of the abuse so as to increase feelings of safety and empowerment.

Therapist focuses on issues the child has brought up—bad dreams about the abuse, fears that the perpetrator will come back, fears that the perpetrators will hurt others, etc. Suggest that the child go through the (memory of past abuse, bad dream, imagined future harm) and change one or more things. The only rule is, "the bad guy or gal can't win." Something must be changed in the story that keeps the perpetrator from hurting the child or those the child loves.

USE YOUR COMMON SENSES

Use your "common senses" to come up with details that make your memory more clear. Relax and take your time!

Sight

Use your eyes
See yourself—how you looked, what you wore (colors and style)
See the place where it happened
See others that were there—how they looked, what they wore
See the action and what happened one thing at a time
See the outdoor surroundings—time of year and weather

Smell

Use your nose
Anything you smelled on a person—breath, sweat, etc.
Anything you smelled at that place

Sounds

Use your ears
Voices—sounds you made/what you said, sounds someone else made/what was said
Other sounds you heard

Touch

What you felt (skin or body): pain, pleasure, rough, gentle, pressure, moisture
Things around you that touched your body
Air temperature—hot and sweaty vs. cold and shivery

Taste

Use your mouth
Anything you tasted
Dry mouth or wet saliva?

Thoughts and Feelings (good or bad: happy, scared, sad, mad, tired, embarrassed, ashamed, guilty, aroused, or whatever)

What you were feeling or thinking before anything happened that day?

What you were feeling or thinking during the abuse?

What you were feeling or thinking after the abuse?

What thoughts or feelings do you have now about what happened?

Did you have dreams about what happened (while you sleep)?

Did things pop into your head about what happened?

MAGIC REMOTE

PLAY

PAUSE

**FAST
FORWARD**

REVERSE

OFF

EJECT

Possible changes to introduce:

1. Move the action to a new place
2. Add an escape or safe place
3. Add a little science fiction or movie magic
4. Call the police, who get there in time to stop the abuse
5. Disable the perpetrator (paralyze, tie up, put in jail, wrap in duct tape, make mute, blast into space, drop by parachute on desert island, weaken with a magic potion, etc.)
6. Make the child a super-hero with special powers to weaken or defeat the perpetrator
7. Bring in a crowd of protective friends
8. Make the perpetrator suffer (cover in honey and biting ants, tar and feather, bury in sand with just his or her head showing in the hot sun)
9. Bring in a helper or super-hero
10. Get the perpetrator to admit what he/she did or write his or her confession
11. Put the perpetrator in a circus with the child as the ringmaster
12. Lock the perpetrator in a zoo cage with the child as the zookeeper
13. Inject humor
14. Turn it into a drama, puppet show, or psychodrama

In lieu of a movie, child and therapist may write a book or create a comic strip of the changed story with the new ending—encourage competency, self-efficacy, and coping skills.

Take-It-Home Discussion Questions

Therapist may assign one or more of the following questions for the child to answer and discuss with parent, foster parent, or staff or prior to the next session.

How am I like Bear?
Who in my life is like Brown Squirrel?
Why did Bear have to tell the whole story?
How do I react when others try to help me?
Is there anything I don't talk about because it is too painful?
Who sticks by me through good and bad times?
How will I feel and act when my "black stuff" is healed?

SYMPTOMS OF PTSD

A therapist may need to educate families and children about PTSD and the types of behaviors and emotional responses children may display following abuse or neglect. Parents and children also need to understand how environmental cues may lead to a recurrence of symptoms long after the original traumatic event(s). The example of an echo may be helpful.

The next story, *Lucky the Junkyard Dog*, is about a victim's response to abuse, including symptoms of PTSD. Later in the story, the dog is triggered again by loud voices, in spite of having been treated well by his new master. This is an excellent story to read in a parents' group, and the participants will identify with various characters in the story.

Lucky was written for a family in which the children had a long history of abuse and neglect. The children were returning home to live with their mother, who had recently moved in with another verbally aggressive, intimidating partner. While not physically abusive, that partner did not understand or believe that his loud voice and intimidation were affecting the children and exacerbating their fear and agitation. This particular stepfather loved dogs and had memories of a beloved pit bull he had rescued. One evening, the author read the story to a parents' group that this man attended.

It was interesting to hear the parents describe their varying responses to the story: "I'm the nice wife," said one mother. "I don't like to see anyone get hurt." Another said, "I'm Lucky at all those different points in his life." The dog turned out to be the connection the stepfather needed to better understand his partner's children. He said, "I'm the mean junkyard man; and I'm Lucky. I grew up that way."

The story of *Lucky* helped these and other parents openly discuss their own upbringing and better understand the effects of their behavior on their children.

LUCKY THE JUNKYARD DOG

Once upon a time there was a two-year-old dog named Lucky who lived with his three brothers and sisters in a dark alley behind the local pool hall. Lucky's mother had been homeless when he was born and she had trouble feeding her large family. She ran around a lot with her friends and wasn't home much. There was never enough food to go around.

Lucky tried to be a good big brother. He loved his brothers and sisters and would protect them at any cost. He let the puppies cuddle around him at night to stay warm; he went hunting for food every night; and he growled at anyone that came too close.

Lucky dreamed of living in a home with a fireplace, a soft bed, a kind master, and a big grassy yard. One day a big man came into the alley and said, "Hey, Joe, there's those wild dogs I talked about. That big one there would make a good guard dog for the junkyard." Before Lucky could growl or run off, the man kicked him hard in the side. Lucky yelped in pain and tried to nip the man in self-defense. The man tossed a rope around his neck, threw him into the back of a red pickup truck, and drove off to the junkyard.

Three years later, Lucky was still living the life of a junkyard dog. The mean junkyard manager kept Lucky on a heavy chain and thought it was funny to tease and torment him. He sometimes held out a juicy steak bone—and when the hungry dog went for it, the man kicked him in the side and pulled it away with a laugh. Lucky could never tell when the man might pet him or when he might curse at him in a loud mean voice and slap him in the head.

The junkyard manager had a wife who was nice to Lucky. But the man hit her too and cursed at her in a loud mean voice. When the man came near her in anger, Lucky tried to protect her by growling and stood between her and the man. She usually pushed Lucky behind her, to keep him safe.

Lucky hated the loud, mean voice and the hitting. He hated hearing the woman shout at the man to get away and really hated hearing her cry when she was hurt.

"You're a good dog, Lucky," the woman said. "Don't you mind him." But Lucky did mind, and he didn't feel like a good dog. He thought there must be something he could do to keep her safe, but he just couldn't figure it out.

Lucky never knew when the man might hurt him. When he heard the man coming, he slunk into the corner with his tail between his legs and growled. When Lucky heard the man shout or curse, he whimpered and stuck his nose between his front paws. He never felt safe and sometimes wished he had never been born.

One day, the junkyard gate opened and a big four-wheel drive pulled in with a load of scrap metal. The junkyard manager had gone to the restroom, so Lucky was alone. "Hey, good buddy," said the man who was unloading his truck. Lucky growled and backed away. The man came a little closer and sounded concerned. "Where did you get all those cuts and bruises, little guy? Your ribs are showing—are you hungry? I have a left-over burger in my truck—would you like it?"

The man went back to his truck to get another load of junk and brought a McDonald's bag with him. "Here you go," he said as he tossed Lucky the burger. Lucky lunged at the treat and gobbled it down. "You're half-starved," said the man. "No one should treat a dog like this."

When the mean junkyard manager came back outside, Lucky growled and slunk away with his tail between his legs. The man raised his leg to kick Lucky, and the nice man said, "Cut that out! You've been beating that dog and he's half-starved. What you're doing is against the law. You're going to let me take that dog with me or I'm going to call the authorities. So what is it? The dog goes with me or I make that call?"

The junkyard man already had a court record, so he unchained Lucky and put him in the man's truck. "You'll be sorry, mister," he said with a sneer. "This mutt ain't going to be no house dog—he has no love in him, just mean-ness."

"We'll see about that," said the nice man as he drove off.

The man drove Lucky to his new home—a nice ranch with a fireplace and a big grassy yard. Lucky ran inside when the man opened the door but headed down to the lower level and slunk into a dark corner. When the man came near him, he growled. The man spoke in a soft, quiet voice, but any minute Lucky expected him to shout, curse, or hit. When the man's wife came to meet Lucky, he wagged his tail a little and stood between her and her husband, baring his teeth.

"That poor dog," said the man's wife. "Let's give him some loving care and time to heal. Maybe he'll learn to trust us."

Lucky didn't trust them. Not even when they gave him a soft bed with a thick blanket. Not even when they fed him treats like steak and liver bits. Not even when they spoke in soft voices. Not even when he realized that his food and water dishes were never allowed to empty.

Finally after quite some time, Lucky realized that the man and woman were *really* nice. They weren't faking it, and they weren't going to hurt him. They gave him a red ball, and every day they took him outside to play. For Lucky, playing was like something from outer space! At first, Lucky hid under the deck—he thought they might throw the ball at him. But one morning he figured out they wanted him to chase and pick it up when they threw it. When he ran after the ball, he heard them laugh and say, "Good boy!" He wagged his tail a little at their praise. Before long, Lucky could not get enough of the "fetch" game.

One day, the man held out a juicy steak bone. "Come here, boy," said the man. Lucky almost growled. Somewhere in his memory was another man holding a steak bone. "It's OK, Lucky. Come get the bone," said the man in a kind voice. Lucky moved, one slow step at a time, toward the nice man. He grabbed the bone in his mouth and ran away with it so that man couldn't hit him or take it back.

"That's the other man," thought Lucky, "but it's hard to forget."

Lucky began to let the man's wife pet him at night before bed. She stroked his scarred back and crooned, "You sweet dog. We are blessed to have you in our lives. We love you!" Lucky liked her gentle, firm touch, and he rolled over to let her pet his belly.

Lucky finally felt safe and loved. He took walks in the neighborhood with the kind master and his wife. He sometimes growled at other people when they came too close, but his master said, "It's OK, Lucky, we won't let anyone hurt you."

One day on a walk, Lucky heard a very loud voice shouting, "You loser! Take your sorry butt back in the house." A very angry big man was raising his fist and shouting at his son. *Instantly*, Lucky's tail went between his legs and he started to growl. The loud voice scared him; and the cursing made him shiver and shake. Lucky pulled away, but his owner held him firmly by the leash.

"No, Lucky, it's OK. Good boy. Sit! Stay!" said his owner in a quiet, firm voice as he reached down to pet him. "You still think something bad might happen to you, but never again. My wife and I will keep you safe. We love you." He stroked Lucky gently on the head and talked to him until he quit shaking.

Then Lucky's owner spoke just loudly enough for the other man to hear him. "That's no way to talk to anyone, and you scared my dog. If you're going to talk like that, take it inside."

The angry man said, "F— you!" but he went in the house and closed the door.

Lucky's owner walked him back home, but Lucky still felt scared. He ran downstairs with his tail between his legs and slunk into the corner. He felt like growling at or biting his owner or the owner's wife. It made no sense, because they were so nice to him. But somewhere in his dog memory, he remembered a loud voice with kicks and hits, and he could almost taste the old pain and fear. He slept downstairs alone that night, ignoring his soft warm bed, and refusing to eat.

Luckily, it didn't take long for the man and his wife to help Lucky through that rough spot, like a bump in the road. Pretty soon he was back to sleeping in his bed and playing in the yard. There were a few more rough spots now and then, but his family was patient—they understood that bad memories last a long time. And every night, as they watched TV, ate popcorn, and fed Lucky dog treats, they said, "Lucky, you are a blessing in our lives!" And every night, right before bed, Lucky rolled over on his back, bared his belly, and whined for just one more petting, please, as he thought, "This is as close to Heaven as it gets!"

THE BOTTOM LINE: Loving care helps but healing takes time!

Treatment Interventions

Family Activity: Match Game

1. Therapist gives each family member a sheet on which the story's characters are listed in a column (see handout on page 28).
2. Therapist asks family members to write their names in a column across from the story characters' column. They may add names of non-family members as desired.
3. Therapist asks family members to draw lines from each person's name to the name of one or more story characters. They are asked to draw a line if the two have something in common.
4. Invite family discussion.

Parent Group Discussion

1. Ask group members who they identified with in the story and why.
2. Ask if any of the group members have had pets. Discuss the ways that humans show empathy for animals.
3. Ask group members if children need the same or different treatment than animals.

PTSD Guided Imagery

This guided imagery may be used to close a group or family session. Therapist reads:

If you live somewhere where there has been a tornado warning, you probably remember what it was like to quickly find a safe place, somewhere with no windows. Right before the warning sounded, the wind blew everything around, the sky got really dark, and it rained very hard. You might have been afraid while hiding and waiting for the storm to pass. Maybe you were prepared for the tornado warning and had a place ready with flashlights, blankets, and a weather radio. Maybe you weren't prepared, and sat in the dark, wondering when it would be over. When it was all over, you probably felt better. But the next time it rained hard, or the wind blew, or the sky got dark, perhaps you were afraid. You might have been afraid there would be another tornado, even if there were no watches or warnings.

Or perhaps you have been in a car accident. After an accident, the details may blur, and you may not even remember exactly what happened. Some people are afraid to get back in the car the next day. Others slow down each time they approach the place the accident occurred. You might have become more watchful and careful when you drove, even if the accident was not your fault.

And if you have not been in a tornado or car accident, you may at least recall a time in your life when things were very stressful. Stress does different things to different people. Perhaps you felt moody or agitated; you might have had trouble sleeping or concentrating. You may have felt all stirred up, like a lake after a storm. After a storm, the sand and water get all mixed in together and lake water becomes very cloudy. It is hard to believe that the water was calm and clear before the storm. It is hard to realize that soon the water will be calm and clear again.

Abuse is a little like that. You may feel all stirred up, even after the abuse stops. And you may or may not have noticed that even long after the abuse is over, things might remind you of past abuse. Like an echo, the memory continues, repeating itself over and over, fainter and fainter, but you can still "hear" and feel it. Hearing an angry voice might stir you up if angry people hurt each another in your home. You might want to fight, protect yourself, or hide in a safe place when you hear a loud, angry voice. If someone touched you a certain way in the past, maybe you don't like anyone to touch you now. Or if your dad got drunk each time he hit your mother, maybe you get nervous now when you smell alcohol on your stepdad's breath.

As long as there is not another storm in the near future, the dirty sand gradually settles down to the bottom of the lake, and the water becomes clear again. It takes time. And after a tornado, car accident, stressful time, or abuse, when you feel all stirred up—give yourself time to settle down.

You may want to focus on the clearing water of the lake, not on the dirt that is settling to the bottom of the lake, since focusing on the water's beauty makes you mindful of your inner peace and serenity. As you picture the lake, fresh and clean once again, perhaps with the sun shining on the surface, your body and mind feel restored, as clear and clean as the lake's blue waters.

Now, as I count from 5 to 1, allow yourself to take a deep, cleansing breath, and gradually open your eyes. 5-4-3-2-1. Fresh, clear, and restored.

Take-It-Home Discussion Questions

Therapist may assign one or more of the following questions for the child to answer and discuss with parent, foster parent, or staff or prior to the next session.

Why was it hard for Lucky to trust his new owners?
How am I like Lucky? Have I ever been treated like Lucky?
Have I ever acted like the first owner?
Which character in the story did you identify with most, and why?
Why did Lucky get scared when he heard the loud arguing during his walk?
Did my mother ever forget to care for me?
Why does it take time to get over abuse?
Who in my life loved/loves me unconditionally?

THE *LUCKY* FAMILY MATCH GAME

List the names of your family members on the right side of the paper. Draw a line between the name of a story character and the name of a family member if they have something in common. You may use some names more than once.

Character Names

Lucky

Lucky's Mother

Junkyard Man

Lucky's Foster Father

Lucky's Foster Mom

Neighborhood Father

Neighborhood Boy

Family Member Names

_____

_____

_____

_____

_____

_____

_____

SIBLING ABUSE

The story *Stick Together* is especially helpful when treating sibling groups that have witnessed abuse or been forced to participate in abuse together. It sends the message that the children in the family are all victims and that no child is "at fault" for what happened at the hands of adults. This story allows siblings to realize that they can "stick together" over what happened to them and understand that they were not to blame.

There are many things parents do that lead siblings to experience animosity toward one another. It is common for abusers to "collude" with one child against another—promising rewards and displaying favoritism. Older children may be forced into vertical relationships with siblings (fear-inducing ones of power and control) while being victimized themselves. Children may be forced to engage in sexual behaviors with siblings or parents; and they may be coerced into unhealthy sleeping arrangements.

Following the initial relief of being "safe" and protected, sibling groups may experience anger or increased arousal in one another's presence and blame one another for the abuse or for "telling" about the abuse. They may move unpredictably from protector, to victim, to perpetrator roles with one another.

This story was written for two brothers, ages 12 and 9, who repeatedly and angrily blamed each other for past abuse. *Stick Together* allows sibling groups to talk about the dangers they faced and create a safe place oasis in which they may stick together, fend off perpetrators, and move forward in recovery. The brothers used the sand tray to create a dangerous desert and labeled "bad guys" with the names of their perpetrators. Over the course of several sessions, they disempowered their perpetrators by burying them, paralyzing them, spinning them inside spider silk, blasting them into space, and wrapping them in duct tape.

Next, they created a safe place oasis. They made it very comfortable and surrounded it with secure gates so that the perpetrators could not get in. The guard was a large snake.

The desert-oasis became their favorite therapeutic intervention and gave them a metaphor that rang true with their prior experience. It allowed them to begin talking about prior unsafe situations and how to feel safe in their new environment.

Children will utilize the story in the ways they most need to address their shared trauma. Therapists are invited to guide them and follow their lead.

STICK TOGETHER

Two iguana brothers lay side by side next to the crystal clear water of the desert oasis, a green and lush haven surrounded by dry, hot sand, as far as you could see. One iguana, Iggy, had a white bandage covering his right foot; the other, Stubby, had a white bandage covering his left foot; and both had cactus quills stuck in their back. They were taking turns biting cactus spines out of each other's backs, going, "Ouch!" and "Hey, that hurt!"

Yes, they had survived a very tough time. As you got closer to them, you could hear them talking. Iggy said to Stubby, "I'll never forget that rattlesnake we came across two nights ago in the desert. He shook those rattles and struck at us before we could even move. I saw his mouth open, and I saw those huge fangs ready to strike, and I knew I was a goner!"

Stubby said, "Yeah, I was sure he was going to get us, so I backed away as fast as I could. And you backed away at the same time, so we bumped into each other. I wish we had seen what was coming!"

"Yup," said Iggy. "What was coming was that huge cactus. After we bumped into each other, we both fell hard on top of it. That hurt like you-know-what!"

Stubby added, "It didn't hurt as much as the scorpion stings did! It wasn't our fault we jumped away from the cactus, and we didn't know the scorpions were sleeping behind it. They sure didn't take kindly to being stepped on!"

For the next week, all the iguanas could think about or talk about was their near-death experience in the desert. They dreamed about it every night, and if either of them heard a noise like a rattle, they jumped two feet in the air and yelled in fear. Iggy and Stubby didn't feel safe, even though there were no rattlesnakes or scorpions at the oasis, so they couldn't appreciate the peaceful surroundings.

The oasis had palm trees with coconuts, fruit trees with apricots, and cool waters to drink. There was shade from the sun and other animals to hang out with, like camels and donkeys. Everyone else at the oasis was having a good old time, but all the iguanas could do was scurry around and talk about rattlesnakes, cactus, and scorpions. They took turns guarding the perimeter of the oasis, to make sure that no rattlesnakes or scorpions entered their territory.

One night when Iggy had a nightmare and couldn't sleep, he nudged Stubby awake and said, "I keep thinking and thinking about *why* this bad luck happened to us and what we could have done to prevent it. There must be a reason." He slowly scratched his bony chin with one clawed foot and continued speaking. "Actually, Stubby, I think it's your fault. If I hadn't been with you, I would have been fine that night. I just know it!"

Stubby replied, "No, you're wrong. My life was fine until that night in the desert. If I hadn't let you talk me into taking a walk out there, it would still be fine. It's all your fault I was in the desert in the first place!"

Iggy retorted, "You're the oldest brother—you're supposed to be on the lookout for danger and keep us safe. You sure messed that up!"

Stubby hollered back, "Well, you know, if you had been looking closer, you might have seen the rattlesnake and warned us. Your eyesight is better than my eyesight. So it's really your fault we fell on the cactus."

Iggy replied in a nasty voice, "If you hadn't been talking so much, I would have seen the cactus and stepped away from it, and then we wouldn't still be picking out stickers."

Stubby retorted in an angry voice, "Well, you might take a little of the blame yourself. When you landed on the cactus you startled me so much with your yell that I jumped up in the air. I came down right on top of that scorpion. It's all your fault I got stung!"

By now, they were both scowling and shouting, and they turned away from each other with a "HMMPHH!"

There they were, two iguanas at a beautiful oasis, and each was trying to blame the other for the past troubles they had shared.

An older iguana had overheard their argument. He approached and asked cautiously, "Do you mind if I make an observation?"

They said it was OK, although they were scowling at one another, and they didn't want to listen to him if it meant they had to quit fighting. The old iguana continued speaking and ignored their scowling faces.

"As I see it, you were at the wrong place at the wrong time. Neither of you is at fault. There wasn't anything either of you could have done to avoid that snake, or the cactus, or the scorpions. Bad things happen to good people. Stuff happens."

"That can't be true," said the iguanas. "There has to be a reason for everything. There must be something we could have done differently."

The older iguana replied, "What happened to you couldn't be helped, but how you get through it is up to you. I suggest you stick together. You both remember what you went through, and you are supposed to be playing on the same team—if you stick together you can win. Hard times come, and hard times go, but it takes an ally to beat the past. By the way, this oasis is a nice place to rest, relax, and get over hard times if you decide to quit blaming each other."

"And," he added, "if you want to blame anyone, blame the snake and the scorpion. They are mean and will strike out at anyone that gets too close."

The iguanas talked about what the older iguana had suggested and called a truce to stop blaming each other and stick together. Iggy and Stubby realized that it was not their fault they got hurt—indeed, the snake and the scorpion would be dangerous to anyone that got too close. They did a pinky swear and began working on a campaign to warn others about the dangers in the desert. They drew warning posters and told their oasis friends about what had happened to them. They didn't want anyone else to get hurt nor did they want desert dangers to enter the oasis.

"It's funny," said Iggy to Stubby one night as he lay by the cool oasis pool and sipped coconut milk. "I couldn't really enjoy the oasis until I stopped worrying about the past."

"Yeah," replied Stubby, giving Iggy a high-five. "I'm glad we talked about it. I doubt we'll ever forget it, but I'm glad we survived it, together!"

THE BOTTOM LINE: Stick together!

Treatment Interventions

Desert and Oasis Activity

1. Ask the child/siblings to draw a picture of the desert and oasis, using dry erase board or mural paper. Take photos.
2. In lieu of drawing, sand table may be used to create a desert/oasis scene. Provide a variety of malevolent characters, water, trees, "good guys," protectors, desert scenery, Lego blocks, duct tape, etc. Engage the children in play therapy once they finish the sand table desert/oasis. Encourage the children to do what they need to do to keep the characters safe in the oasis. Children are likely to disable the perpetrators in some way or build a safety barrier.
3. Invite the children to discuss who in the desert caused the most harm or fear. Discuss what happened to the "good" characters in the desert and how they got away. Who in the oasis can be trusted? Who in their life caused harm/fear? Who do they trust?
4. Ask them how they can keep the oasis safe and how they will respond if desert characters try to breach the oasis perimeter. How will the characters stick together?
5. Help children do such things as make warning signs, carry out a "protest march" against child abuse, publish a list of dangerous desert characters, and make "wanted" posters.
6. Continue to use the desert and oasis theme in play therapy across a number of sessions, drawing out details and linking the play to the child's own life experiences. Therapist may ask siblings how they will stay safe and "stick together."

Take-It-Home Discussion Questions

Therapist may assign one or more of the following questions for the child to answer and discuss with parent, foster parent, or staff or prior to the next session.

What can I do to stick together with my brother/sister?
What was hardest to survive in the desert of my life?
What do I think about the phrase "stuff happens"?
What can we enjoy about being together in the oasis?
How do I feel about the fact that bad things happen to good people?

RESIDUAL EFFECTS OF TRAUMA

The following story of a poisonous spider, told by a six-year-old abuse victim during the termination process, is about breaking free from the cycle of abuse and finding hope.

This story suggests that abuse *changes* the victim and that trusting, unconditional relationships help victims heal. The story's action *seeds* self-efficacy and trust.

The story will be thought provoking for adults that believe traumatized children should have better self-control and "forget about" the past. There is a strong metaphor in the story—that trauma is a poison that seeps into the child's innermost self, leading him or her to strike out in anger at those who try to help.

Family or group members will easily move into a treatment activity after they hear this story. There is no *right* activity—therapists may follow the lead of the clients or come prepared to lead an activity. Activities generally focus on trust, healing, passing on "poison," and finding hope.

THYME TO HEAL

A large, beautiful blue spider with red specks inside was spinning a delicate web underneath a garden bench. As a woman approached the bench, the spider gave her a curious glance—she had never seen a woman with orange-colored lava hair, hands with magic wand tips, and heart-shaped chocolate buttons on her dress. The woman also gave a curious glance at the spider, because she had never seen a blue garden spider with red specks inside.

The woman sat down on the bench to rest and said, "Hello, spider, what's up with you?" She added, "My name is Hope. What's yours?"

The spider replied, "My name is Lydia." And, then, a little sadly, "You better stay back. I'm full of red poison, and if you get too close, I might bite you. I don't want to bite you, but if I get the urge to bite, I will bite. And if I bite you, my poison will make you sick."

The woman said, "Why are you full of poison? Garden spiders usually aren't poisonous."

The spider replied, "You're right, they usually aren't. My mother was a beautiful, poison-free garden spider. But something went wrong after I hatched from her egg, and I became a poisonous garden spider instead of a harmless garden spider. Now no one wants to come near me, because it's not safe."

The woman stated, "No one wants to get bitten by a poisonous spider. Can't you just use some self-control?"

"Unfortunately," said the spider, "whatever filled me with poison also made me want to bite and hurt others. The strong urge to bite comes over me, and I bite before I even have time to think about it. After I bite, I'm very sorry, and then I swear I'll never do it again. But sooner or later, the urge comes back, and I bite someone else. I've learned to not make any promises."

"You know," she added, "pretty soon it will be time for me to lay my first spider egg. I don't want to pass the poison on to my baby. What am I to do?"

"I'm not sure what you can do," said the woman. "Let me think about it for a few days."

Several days later, the woman came walking down the path. "Spider, oh, spider . . ." called the woman.

"Here I am," said the spider, perched in a beautiful web above the path.

"Come down," said the woman. "I found the answer to your question, and I think I can help you."

"Please tell me," said the spider.

"It won't be easy," the woman replied. "I need to be sure you are ready to take the first step."

"I'm ready," said the spider. "It is Thyme to Heal, for the sake of my baby and all my children to come."

"OK," said the woman. "When it is Thyme to Heal, and a full moon night, a spider can get rid of her poison by working with a healer. I am a healer, and I can work with you."

"What great news!" the spider replied. "Please tell me what we need to do!"

The woman continued. "First, stay away from others until you are poison-free. Oh, not totally away. Just keep outside your striking distance. That way, you won't poison anyone, especially your friends. Others need to be safe when you're around."

"That sounds good," said the spider. "I don't even trust myself, so I'll keep my distance. I can warn my friends if they come too close."

"Next," continued the woman, "on a full-moon night, right before you lay your first spider egg, if I wave my magic wand hands over your head ten times the poison will go away. You have to remain very still while I do that, to allow the magic to work. For the magic to work, you have to believe that you will heal. When we're done, I feed you a little thyme, a tasty herb, to keep you poison-free. Once you are poison-free, your first baby, born from your first egg, will be poison-free. I will have to get close to you, though, so I take a risk that you might bite me before I can work the spell."

"Are you sure you want to do that?" asked the spider.

"Yes, I'm sure," said the woman. "You're worth the risk."

They said good-bye, and the spider promised to find the woman on the next full-moon night when she was ready to lay her first egg.

About a week later, the spider came back to the garden to find the woman. It was going to be a full-moon night, and the spider was ready to lay her first egg. "Yoo-hoo!" called the spider. "Hey, lava-hair woman, it's me, your spider friend!"

The woman stepped out of the forest, her lava hair glowing bright orangish-red in the light of the rising moon. "It's time," said the spider. "If we don't do it tonight, it will be too late. I'll try hard not to bite you when you come near me, but I can't make any promises."

"OK," said the woman with the lava hair. "Perhaps the warmth of my lava hair will make you sleepy and keep you from biting me."

"I hope so," said the spider.

So the woman moved toward the spider. Just before she reached the spider, she pulled off two of her sweet chocolate buttons and threw them in the spider's mouth.

"Mmmmm!" said the spider as she chewed the sweet chocolate. And at just that moment, the woman moved closer and waved her magic wand hands over the spider's head. She kept waving her hands until she had waved them ten times. The spider felt a quick surge of great pain while the woman waved her magic wand hands over the spider's head, followed by warm glow that spread through her body and mind. "I believe," she thought. "I believe that I will be healed!"

"There," said the woman. But as the woman pulled her magic wand hands away from the spider, the spider lunged at the woman and bit down hard with her fangs on one of the woman's hands.

"Owww!" cried the woman in pain, rubbing her hand.

"Oh no!" said the spider. "I'm so sorry! I tried hard not to bite you, but I got the urge and just could not resist. Are you OK?"

"I suspected you would do that," said the woman with a gentle smile. "It is your nature to bite. But when you bit me, the poison left you. Your poison can't hurt me. My magic wand hands protect me and keep poison from reaching my heart. And, my friend, you are poison-free!"

It was true. The red specks had disappeared—the poison was gone!

The woman said, "Now open your mouth, and I'll throw in a little thyme. That will *keep* you poison-free!" The spider opened her mouth wide, and avoiding the sharp fangs, the woman threw in a little thyme.

As she bid the spider farewell, the woman said, "Go to sleep, spider, and when you wake back up, you will have a new egg."

The spider fell into a deep sleep. Hours later, she awoke, refreshed. On the ground next to her was a brand new egg, her first egg and baby-to-be. What an amazing sight it was, striped with all the colors of the rainbow! It was clearly a very special egg, full of new life, and she could not wait for it to hatch.

When it was time, the egg hatched, and there was her baby garden spider, bright blue and poison-free. The spider knew that she would teach her baby many things and that they would live a poison-free life together. She named the baby Hope, after the woman with the lava hair and magic wand hands. The spider realized she did not really know or care whether it was the woman's kindness or her own willingness to trust that had made the magic work and allowed her to heal.

We all have a little poison inside us—maybe you can find a healer to help you get rid of your poison. And once you are poison-free, do whatever you need to do to give birth to your own Hope.

THE BOTTOM LINE: Give birth to something remarkable!

Treatment Interventions

Family Drawing

This may also be done with an individual or group.

1. Therapist tells the family (or group) their task is to work together to draw a mural.
2. Explain to the family that each person was affected differently by the family experiences.
3. Like the spider in the story, each has something negative inside that may feel like "poison"—something that wasn't in there before the abuse or neglect and something they want to heal.
4. Ask the family to draw a large spider and fill it with poison that came from negative or unpleasant family experiences. Each can add his or her own "poison" to the drawing. Discuss each family member's poison, what it feels like, and why he or she wants to get rid of or heal it.
5. Ask the family members to draw a giant egg. Each should draw something inside the egg that stands for his or her hope. It can be a hope for the individual or hope for the family. Define hope as one or more changes that will take place after they heal, i.e., when there is no longer abuse or neglect in their lives.

Take-It-Home Discussion Questions

Therapist may assign one or more of the following questions for the child or parent to answer and discuss.

Parent
As I think about my upbringing, what were good things I want to pass on to my children ("hope")?
What were things I don't want to pass on to my children ("poison")?
What negative behaviors have I "copied" from my parents?

Child or Parent
How does the spider feel when the woman says, "You're worth it"? How do I feel when someone says that to me?
What are some remarkable things about me?
Who in my life accepts my bite and still loves me?

2

Establishing Appropriate Roles and Boundaries in Families

It was an interesting session of group therapy for abused and neglected youth. "When I was 8," said one 11-year-old proudly, "I got up at night and fed my brother his bottle. Then I changed his diaper!"

Another stated, "My 10-year-old brother took good care of us when my mommy left for the night. He fed us and made us go to bed on time. If we were bad, he gave us time-out or made us go to bed early. I went in my room and pretended my mommy was in the other room watching TV. Then I could go to sleep."

In one family, "time-out" included locking the children in a dark closet overnight and putting them in their rooms for long periods of time. In another family, the mother allowed the children to pick who she could date.

Families that experience abuse, neglect, or domestic violence often develop inappropriate relationship boundaries. Victims of domestic violence, abuse, or neglect often tend to the needs of others at their own expense and become codependent. Such persons may have been raised in families with substance abuse or domestic violence. Partners of or children of substance abusers abdicate their own needs and enable or rescue others in order to keep peace or survive. A codependent mother "sacrifices" herself to her partner's demands. Above all, she wants to be seen as a loving mother but she confuses loving with giving in. Life becomes one day of walking on thin ice after another.

There are a number of ways in which boundaries become confused. Children may take on adult roles, and adults may relate to their children as friends or peers. Child rearing practices may be over- or under-protective, guided by cross-generational "truisms" or cultural beliefs.

Therapists working with victims of abuse or neglect should carefully assess family boundaries, discipline practices, assigned responsibilities (such as chores), and parental expectations for things such as privileges (bedtime, dating, movies/TV). Parents in these families have little idea of what is developmentally age-appropriate. Parents may give too many or too few choices. Older children may be expected to care for younger children, and force and intimidation may be considered "discipline."

One mother reunifying with her children discussed her private adult life with her teenage daughter ("I'm not going to lie to her"), not understanding that this would affect her daughter's view of her as a mother. Another client's mother had never told her that her father, who left the family when she was two, was gay; and when he died of AIDS it was devastating news.

A child's developmental age and stage affects his or her response to abuse or neglect. Parents may not realize that as children reach new developmental levels, they will have new or different concerns about prior abuse. Parents may believe that once children have discussed the abuse, it will not (and need not) come up again. Some parents or family members discourage their children from talking about prior abuse, since "they should be over it by now" and "things in the past should be left in the past." Parents need to be educated about the recurrent nature of abuse issues and encouraged to listen and be supportive.

Abusive and neglectful parents display deficits in their *scaffolding* ability (Morelock et al. 2003). Scaffolding is when a skilled and sensitive parent challenges a child to do things just outside that child's current skill level. Abusive or neglectful parents may not know how to adjust their behaviors to match a child's needs. They expect children to be able to do things far beyond their current capacities or overprotect and do not allow children to do age-appropriate things.

This author recently observed the mother of a 19-month-old and 7-year-old as the baby kicked at the older child's feet and toys. When asked why the mother did not step in to redirect or distract the baby she replied that someone had suggested she let her (older) children work out problems among themselves before she stepped in. This mother had generalized what she had been told, not realizing that a 19-month baby was incapable of this level of problem solving.

A young mentally ill mother who had abused her 3-month old baby said, "That baby got on my last nerve—it knew I wanted to sleep and was crying to get me mad!" The mother was convinced that the baby could tell what she was feeling and engaging in purposeful action.

There are many excellent books and websites for parents that address child development, appropriate play behavior, and positive discipline, and parents referred to treatment benefit from psycho-educational classes in these areas. The goal of this chapter is not to *educate* but, rather, to help parents pay better attention to and respond differently to their children's developmental abilities and limitations.

AGE-APPROPRIATE EXPECTATIONS

The story that follows, *Velma Crowe's Sticky Situation*, suggests that parents raised under less-than-ideal circumstances may have unusual views of how to raise children. Velma was modeled on mothers whose problems *blind* them to seeing their children's needs and prevent them from putting the children's needs before their own.

It is an excellent story for a parenting group, as parents are likely to laugh as they recognize themselves and their own parents in the antics of this feathered friend.

Once parents read this story, there are two ways to approach discussion. The first is how they as children might have experienced their parents' behavior. The second is how their own parental behavior impacts their children.

The Velma story is equally effective in a child group or family therapy session, where participants will share views of what children need to grow up healthy and to feel loved.

VELMA CROWE'S STICKY SITUATION

Velma Crowe lives in Bird Town, a very nice place to live if you are a bird. The town is full of trees, with birdhouses and bird feeders in every tree, and a lake beyond the trees for bathing. The ground in Bird Town is full of worms and grubs, and there are plenty of crickets and bugs. Every morning at dawn, you can hear the Bird Town Chorus singing bird songs as the sun rises. What more could you ask for, if you were a bird?

Well, Velma could have asked for more. She had been different from other Bird Town birds since the day she was hatched—a mutant misfit. Poor Velma was born with *feathers* on her wings! Isn't that the oddest thing you ever heard? Well, for Bird Town it is. Do you want to guess what the birds in Bird Town are covered with? No, it isn't cat fur or plastic wrap or suction cups or cotton balls. It's that stuff some people have on the straps of their tennis shoes, to strap them shut instead of using shoe laces.

Yes, humans call it Velcro, but not the residents of Bird Town, who are such bird brains. They call it Skritch, because when you pull the sides apart, you hear a very annoying loud *SKRITCH*! It's a sound that teachers HATE—they probably wish everyone had shoelaces.

In Bird Town, after the eggs hatch, baby birds launch themselves at their mother and stick to her. What an adorable sight—little birds, securely attached to their mother, chirping loudly to be fed. Baby birds in Bird Town don't have to worry where their next meal will come from—their mother hears them chirping and drops yummy, partially digested worms right into their open beaks. Day and night the babies are safe, right under the mother's watchful eye.

Velma Crowe's brothers and sisters teased her for being different, as brothers and sisters often do.

"No-stick Velma wants to play, come again some other day!"

Velma got banged up a lot when she flung herself at her mother and slid to the ground. Her brothers and sisters got most of the worms with their mother's help, so Velma was hungry all the time as a baby. She often got lost in the woods when she wandered off.

Over time, Velma learned to take care of herself. She bought a pair of glasses, because she could not see very well, and found her own worms in the wet, early morning grass. With her glasses on, she watched for possible dangers in the forest, because her mother was often too far away to keep her safe. And even though she was tone deaf (which meant she sang out of tune), she sang with great enthusiasm in the Bird Town Chorus.

Velma finally grew up, but even as an adult she had problems. She didn't pay close attention to things and was accident prone—one minute she would be flying toward a tree and the next minute she would forget about the tree and fly right into it. *Plop*!

Velma didn't *like* having feathers, but she wouldn't admit that to anyone. Velma was a tough old bird, meaning she usually pretended that things didn't bother her and hid her hurt feelings. "I've always been different," she said. "They can take it or leave it."

To take her mind off her problems, Velma went out and had a lot of fun. She partied and drank nectar with her friend Hummingbird, who didn't care about Velma's feathers. They danced late into the night at the Bird Town Disco. Every Friday night Velma went to late-night karoake with her friend Hound Dog. Hound Dog could really howl up a storm to the music!

But now Velma was going to become a mother. She had laid five eggs in a nest, and soon the eggs were going to hatch.

Hummingbird and Hound Dog were concerned about Velma and decided to talk to her. They knew that baby birds would bring change into the life of their fun-loving friend. That Friday night, Hummingbird and Velma flew to the club and sipped nectar as Hound Dog howled out a great rendition of "Proud Mary."

Hummingbird said, "Vel, you'll need to change your lifestyle when your babies hatch. You know, settle it down a little."

"Nah," said Vel, taking a sip of nectar. "I can have babies and have fun too!"

"You'll be a *mother*, Vel," replied Hummingbird. "You can have fun, but you'll need to put your family first."

"I'll be a good mother," said Velma. "There's nothing to it!"

Hound Dog returned to the table after a round of applause. "We were just talking about Velma becoming a mother," said Hummingbird.

Hound Dog said, "I've been told that babies like to snuggle up close to their mothers while they eat and sleep. Yours won't be able to do that because your feathers are too slippery."

Velma replied, "I've never been the cuddly type."

Hummingbird asked, "What are you going to do when the babies can't attach to you? Aren't you worried about what might happen to them?"

"Nonsense," said Velma. "They'll have to learn to hang on, because if they can't hang on, they'll be on their own."

"But baby birds can't take care of themselves," said Hound Dog. "You will need to feed them and keep them safe."

"I'm sure they'll be fine," said Velma. "No one took very good care of me, and I turned out OK, didn't I?"

"No comment!" said both Hummingbird and Hound Dog, at the same time.

Velma returned to her nest about 2 AM, and an hour later the eggs hatched—five beautiful baby birds emerged.

"Climb on," said Velma to her babies. "We're going out to eat to celebrate your birthday!"

The babies, like all baby birds in Bird Town, were covered in Skritch. They flung themselves at their mother, seeking a place to stick, their little feet gripping her feathers. No such luck.

"Sliiiide, thunk. Sliiide, thunk. Sliiide, thunk. Sliiide, thunk. Sliiide, thunk."

Five baby birds slid off their mother and dropped to the ground below.

"Look at that!" said Velma fondly. "Those little buggers are accident prone, just like their mother."

At that, the baby birds began to cry and chirp—it hurts to fall on the hard ground, and they were very hungry. "Chirp, chirp, chirp," cried her five complaining children. Velma hunted for some worms but could only feed one baby at a time. "You'll have to wait your turn," she said to one particularly loud baby. "I can't feed all five of you at once!"

The babies kept trying to attach to Velma, jumping on her and then falling back to the ground. Velma finally used her wings to brush them away. Once the babies realized they were not going to stick to Velma, they started to explore. Velma saw five baby birds hopping off in five different directions.

"Oh look," she said. "My babies are independent—just like me! Don't go too far," she called out. She pointed with her wing. "There's a mean owl that lives over there in an old tree. Stay away from it if you can."

The five baby birds did what babies do—they continued to cry, with their hungry mouths open, and they did not listen to their mother. All five hopped away.

"Oh well," said Velma. "What can you do when your children won't listen to you? I guess they'll learn from life's experiences, just like I did—the school of hard knocks!"

Velma gave up trying to keep the babies near her. She was so tired from flying around and feeding five busy baby birds. She settled on a tree limb to rest for a minute—her head dropped down onto her wing, and soon she fell sound asleep.

As if out of a fog, Velma heard, "Velma, wake up! Where are your babies? The nest and eggs are empty!"

She woke up to find Hound Dog standing over her.

"Did you say something?" asked Velma. "Why did you wake me? I was up all night and need to catch up on my sleep!"

"Where are your babies?" asked Hound Dog with concern in his voice. "You can't sleep while they are up and around. You need to keep an eye on them!"

Velma rubbed the sleep out of her eyes and said, "Don't look so worried. I'm sure they are fine. They can pretty well take care of themselves."

"You're wrong," said the Hound Dog. "Baby birds need constant care and protection."

"It's not my fault," said Velma. "They won't stick to or listen to me. What do you expect me to do?"

"I'll get back to you after I find the babies," said Hound Dog, who began sniffing around. Within a few minutes, he found all five baby birds. He gently picked them up in his slobbery mouth and carried them back to their mother.

"Velma," said Hound Dog, "you don't know how to take care of your babies. We need to figure something out so that you can be a good mother and keep your babies safe."

Hound Dog ran off sniffing at the ground, because that is what hound dogs do when they are trying to solve a problem. Soon he returned, carrying a large package in his mouth.

"What's that you're carrying?" asked Velma.

Hound Dog ripped open the package. Inside was a coat, labeled, "Bird Skritch Coat—Guaranteed to Stick!" The coat was covered in Skritch, and it zippered up the front so it wouldn't come off.

"Try wearing this," said Hound Dog. "Keep it where you'll remember to wear it. We both know you have trouble remembering things. See if it works for you and the babies. After all, their needs come first at this stage of their lives."

Velma put on the Skritch coat, one wing at a time, and zipped it up tightly. "OK, kids," she said, "climb aboard!"

The baby birds flung themselves at her.

"Skritch-stick. Skritch-stick. Skritch-stick. Skritch-stick. Skritch-stick," went the baby birds as they attached to her coat. They chirped happily as they snuggled into Velma.

"I don't know about this," said Velma. "I won't have much privacy when they are right here beneath my beak."

"Well, they need to be where you can keep an eye on them, until they're a little older," said Hound Dog. "You can't let babies get too far away—they explore and get into things that can hurt them."

It was a very looong week. Velma wasn't used to having little or no time to herself and being surrounded by babies.

"Chirp, chirp, chirp," they went, day and night, except for when they were sleeping. They were always hungry, and Velma could not get a full night's sleep.

A week later, Velma met up with Hound Dog. She looked very tired, with circles under her eyes.

"Hound Dog," said Velma, "those babies cry day and night. I never get a full night's sleep. They wake me up too early and won't go back to sleep. All that crying really gets on my nerves."

"All babies cry," said Hound Dog. "That's what babies do. You have to be patient. Believe it or not, they cry less if you take good care of them."

"I'll take your word for it," Velma replied. "I guess life's hard enough without having to find your own food or take care of yourself when you're little."

Velma got used to having noisy babies around day and night. She slept when they slept and took them with her wherever she went. When she wanted a night out, she hired Grandma Hound Dog, a reliable baby-sitter. And even when the babies woke her up too early, she got up with them. She fed them worms when they were hungry and played with them when they chirped for her to pay attention to them.

Hound Dog was right. Her babies depended on her to care for them. She knew when they were older they would all leave the nest, and then she would have more time for herself.

It would be worth waiting for.

THE BOTTOM LINE: Help children attach (in one way or another!).

Treatment Interventions

Stick, Babies, Stick!

1. Using Ping-Pong balls covered in Velcro, create baby birds by drawing on beaks, eyes, and wings in permanent marker.
2. Ask participants to discuss why mothers must keep their babies near them.
3. Using a large piece of cardboard or poster board, draw Velma without her Skritch coat.
4. Give out the babies—ask participants to throw them at Velma and see if they will stick.
5. Glue some Velcro on Velma. Let participants throw the babies at Velma and see them stick.
6. Gradually increase distance from Velma and see how far away the babies can get before they will no longer stick.
7. Discuss how far away babies or children can get from their parents (at each age of development) before it is no longer safe. Ask participants what can happen when children are not kept close at hand.
8. Discuss places that children can safely or not safely go without their parents.

Role Reverse (Parenting Group)

1. In a parenting group, ask parents to split into two groups. One group will play children and the other will play parents.
2. Tell the *children* to each write down something their own children have done that was unwise, unsafe, or not age-appropriate. Put the slips of paper in a container.
3. Tell the *parents* to "go to sleep."
4. Have the *children* pick a behavior out of the container. While the parents sleep, the children get into a little trouble and act out the unsafe behavior.
5. "Wake up" the parents. Have the *children* tell the parents what they did while the parents slept.
6. Ask the parents to respond inappropriately (they may blame the *children* for what happened, excuse it, ignore it, encourage it, or minimize it).
7. Ask the *children* what they thought of the parents' response.
8. *Children* pick next situation and act it out while parents sleep.
9. After playing out a few "inappropriate parent responses," ask the *children* to act out a situation while the parents group stays awake and sets limits or prevents the children from carrying out their plan.

10. *Children* give the parents feedback about how this is different than the other situations.
11. Pick a new situation and repeat, with parents awake and giving appropriate response.

Bird School for Velma

1. Tell parent/child group or family that Velma is being sent to Bird Town parenting classes.
2. Ask participants to break into small groups and select behaviors that they would want to address in parenting class: attitudes, beliefs, and behaviors. Why do they select those?
3. Ask participants to create lesson plans for Velma that will teach her some new attitudes, beliefs, and behaviors.
4. Present the different lesson plans to the group/family.
5. Carry out the lesson plan, using participants as teachers and Velma the puppet as the student.

Take-It-Home Discussion Questions

Therapist may assign one or more of the following questions for the child or parent to answer and discuss with parent, foster parent, or therapist.

Who does Velma remind me of?
When have I acted like Velma?
Did anyone act like Velma with me? What did they do?
When do I have trouble putting my children's needs before my own?

3

The *Fight* of Fight or Flight

Self-Control and Modulation of Affect

Anger is triggered easily in some traumatized individuals, whose neurobiology and cognitive/emotional filtering lead to faulty perception and heightened reactivity. Through the experience of abuse, they develop negative schemas and later become easily upset by life events that resemble those they experienced in the past.

Angry individuals may perceive threats to safety when none are present or project malevolent intentions onto others. They move quickly into *fight* in order to self-protect. Because they misread social cues, they do not accurately perceive the intentions and behaviors of others. Quick to perceive hostile intent, they are likely to attack ("I'll get you before you get me!") or retaliate even when no danger is present. A necessary component of therapy is cognitive restructuring, whereby the child develops cognitive evaluation skills and improves self-control.

Many traumatized children get diagnosed with bipolar or mood disorder NOS due to the intensity of their outbursts; yet their symptoms may be better understood and addressed within a trauma continuum model.

Ross Greene's book *The Explosive Child* (2001) describes the reactivity of explosive children. According to Dr. Greene, explosive children do not respond well to behavioral consequences due to the extreme nature of their outbursts and their lack of connection between behavior and consequence. When the limbic areas of the brain are activated during an outburst, a traumatized child is *unable* to think. Often, children with affect regulation problems, especially those with multiple traumas, will require pharmacological treatment. It is hard to use your brain for problem solving when the pre-frontal cortex is disengaged.

Adults need to help children calm themselves when they are becoming angry, before they reach peak levels of arousal, so that they retain the capacity to process, think, and plan, i.e., ability to use the pre-frontal cortex areas of the brain. A raging child has already moved biologically to survival mode, which precludes thinking and reasoning.

When a potentially explosive child starts to lose control, anything that reduces the child's physiological arousal (de-escalates) may be helpful, such as music, walking, rocking, art, and relaxation techniques. Active listening, redirection, distraction, and empathy also may prevent a full-blown meltdown when a child is showing early signs of emotional upset. If an adult belittles the child's concern, gets into power struggles, or argues with the child, the child is more likely to fight or withdraw. Dr. Greene suggests that adults not try to reason with, threaten, warn, or talk to children who are in the midst of emotional storms.

Children engage in aggressive behavior for a variety of reasons. Some children bully or fight with others to be in control and avoid getting hurt. For such children, it is safer (and more comfortable) to be the aggressor than the victim. Therapy helps these children learn how to be safe in more appropriate ways and that it is not OK for them to be hurt by or to hurt others.

Other children may be depressed following abuse and display symptoms of irritability and argumentativeness. They are sensitive and self-critical, and become easily angered when they believe others are criticizing them. Depressed children draw the wrong conclusions from what others say, and they misinterpret social cues.

One six-year-old had grown up in a family where family members called names, cursed loudly, accused people of bad intentions, and blamed others for mistakes. She believed that almost all behavior toward her was of malevolent intent and cursed at others loudly with little provocation. Eventually, as people treated her kindly on a consistent basis, she began to interact more appropriately and display empathy toward other children in the group home.

There are some children that engage in malicious and coercive behaviors toward others. They seem to "enjoy" hurting or victimizing younger children and have little empathy. They threaten peers (often targeting weaker individuals) and escalate to get adults to give in or back down—*a controlled out of control*. Caregivers need to recognize the difference between angry coercion that *holds people hostage* versus a true loss of control.

Children that witness domestic violence may develop anger-management problems. They feel powerless seeing their mother get hurt as well as guilty that they can't stop it; they dislike living in an abusive environment; and they don't really understand why their mother stays with such a hurtful partner. Some jump in as the mother's protector, acting older than their age. When a child protector becomes a teenager, he or she may become angry to avoid feelings of vulnerability and take the anger out on the mother, while displaying disdain and lack of respect. A mother may begin to see similarities between her son and her partner and conclude, "He's just like his (abusive) father." The risk is that the mother will respond to her son as she did her abuser, by doing such things as tolerating abuse, withholding affection, aggressing in return, and becoming judgmental or rejecting. A mother that has not dealt with her own abuse issues is likely to have difficulty dealing with the anger displayed by her children.

It is important that adults hold children *accountable* for the times when they hurt others. Once a child calms down (perhaps later that day or the next day) a parent and child may explore the sequence of events, so that the child learns new coping techniques and ways to avoid triggers in the environment. If a parent or caregiver is going to give a consequence for the behavior, he or she needs to give it after the child has calmed down. Ideally, the consequence will be a teaching consequence that is connected to what the child did. For example, a child can help repair a hole in the wall that he or she made or forfeit part of his or her allowance to cover the cost of damages.

Most children feel remorseful after an angry outburst—they regret things they said and did while angry. Following an outburst, a child needs time to regain control, a chance to debrief or process, and an opportunity to make amends. Children don't want to alienate those they care about—they desire restitution and reconciliation. Parents need to be able to forgive and *wipe the slate clean*. It should be noted, however, that some children apologize in order to *get out of* a consequence. Step-by-step processing will help such a child learn accountability.

Parents need to be accountable for their own angry behavior. They need to not excuse their behavior or the behavior of their partners. A parent that has lost control (said and done things that were not appropriate) needs to admit this to the children, express remorse, and begin using new coping techniques. Angry behavior can be very hurtful and destructive—after all, it is not anger that destroys; it is the way it is displayed in behavior.

The stories and interventions in this section target anger management. The interventions may be used in conjunction with mindfulness techniques to provide some psychological distance and with cognitive behavioral techniques for anger management.

SELF-CONTROL

The first story in this chapter, *Keep Your Lion on a Leash!*, is a helpful metaphor about self-control and what happens when anger is *unleashed*.

Children (and their parents) must be able to control their actions when angry. A therapist may use this story as a lead-in to work on anger-management issues.

The little boy in this story is a precocious, strong-minded child who struggles, as many children do, between the desire to please and comply with his mother, and the desire to follow his own impulses.

It is important to note that the solution in this story is not for the little boy to blindly obey or get rid of the lion. The solution to the story is one of balance, whereby children can be free to make some decisions on their own, while considering risks.

The metaphor of the unleashed lion encourages children to modulate strong affect so that it does not destroy them or others.

KEEP YOUR LION ON A LEASH!

Sam really liked to do things his own way. He just couldn't help it. His mother would say, "Please don't wipe your mouth on your shirt when you're eating." But Sam really *liked* wiping his mouth on his shirt. For one thing, the napkin took too much time. He also liked how all the food colors looked on his shirt—like a piece of art! So when his mother wasn't looking, he wiped his mouth on his shirt. Sometimes his mother caught him doing it and said, "Oh, Sam, you always want to do things your own way." It was true—he was just that kind of boy.

By the way, did I tell you that Sam had a pet lion that lived in his bedroom? He got it for his birthday when it was just a baby. "That's it!" Sam had thought. "I'll call him Baby!" The baby lion liked to run around Sam's room, and Sam taught him how to wrestle. What a fun pet to play with! It hid in Sam's closet and jumped out at him—"Peek-A-Boo!" Baby purred real loud, too, like a motor running—he could feel it on his cheek when the lion cuddled up beside him to watch TV in his bedroom. Sam taught Baby tricks, like "stand up" and "beg for hot dogs." Baby listened to him better than the dog did!

As Sam grew, Baby grew, too. Soon, Baby was really BIG (his mouth was as big as Sam's head) and Sam's mother said, "Baby is so big now that you must keep him on a leash. He is a wild creature and doesn't know his own strength. He will hurt you or someone else without meaning to."

"Oh, Mom," said Sam, rolling his eyes. "Baby is my friend, and he loves me. He would never hurt me."

"Trust me, Sam," answered his mother. "Baby is a lion, and it is his nature to hunt and attack. I want you to buy a leash today. If you let him off the leash, you won't be able to control him."

Sam didn't want to admit it, but he was a little afraid of Baby now. Baby was bigger than Sam, and his teeth and claws were sharp and pointed. When Baby *ROARED*, he scared everyone in the house. So Sam decided to listen to his mother and bought a bright red collar and a nice strong leash. From that day on, Sam kept Baby on the leash. He still made him do tricks, like fetch the dog (just kidding!!), and Baby still lay next to him and purred when they watched TV together in Sam's room.

But a part of Sam still wanted to do it *his way*—after all, Baby was his friend. He kind of let himself forget what his mother had said. He thought, "What Mom doesn't know won't hurt her. I'll try letting Baby off the leash for a few minutes. I trust Baby—I don't think he would ever hurt me!"

Sam looked Baby in the eye and quickly unhooked the leash from the lion's collar when his mother wasn't looking. "Good lion," said Sam. But Baby opened his mouth and *ROARED* with a loud mean rumble. Sam backed away and said, "STAY, BABY!" Baby moved forward slowly, one step at a time, a wild look in his eye. The hair on the back of his neck stood up, his tail went up in the air, and his eyes narrowed. He looked like a wild lion! Baby swiped at Sam with a huge clawed paw and squatted down like he was ready to pounce.

Sam thought, "Oops, bad decision . . ." He saw how dangerous and wild Baby was off the leash. Sam did not know what to do, because any minute now he was going to get eaten alive! Then Sam had a sudden "AHA." He ran out of his room and slammed the door behind him. "ROAR," went Baby, as he clawed at the door. It was a very thick door, so for the moment, Sam was safe.

Sam dashed into the kitchen and grabbed ten hot dogs out of the fridge. Baby *loved* hot dogs! But as Sam headed back down the hall toward his room, he saw his mother at his bedroom door, her hand on the doorknob. "What is all the noise in there?" Sam heard his mother say as she turned the doorknob. "Oh NO!" thought Sam. "Mom is going to get eaten alive!" He *shouted*, "MOM, DON'T OPEN THE DOOR!"

But it was too late! The door started to open. "ROAR!" Baby's head pushed out through the crack—so close that Sam's mother could feel his hot breath on her hand. She saw Baby's head just in time and managed to get the door closed before the lion could take a bite out of her. Her face was quite red and she did not look very happy. Sam's mother backed away from the door and said sternly, her hands on her hips, "Sam, what have you done? That lion is off his leash!"

Sam did not answer her. He quickly opened his bedroom door a crack and threw the ten hot dogs far into the room, behind Baby. When the lion turned around to eat them, Sam jumped into the room and quickly re-hooked the leash to Baby's collar. Then Sam commanded, "BABY, STAY!" as he tugged on the leash, and Baby lay down with his head on his paws. He looked a little sad, as if to say, "Sam, I didn't want to hurt you or your mother. It is just my nature."

Sam ran over to where his mother was standing. "Mom, let me explain," he begged. His mother shook her head "No" and held out her hand like a stop sign. "Oh boy," thought Sam, "I'm in real trouble, now." His mother said, "Give me a minute, Sam. My heart is pounding and I need to calm down." Her face was still quite red.

In a few minutes, his mother had calmed back down. She said, "Sam, I know you like to do things your way, but doing things your way this time almost got us killed."

Sam replied, "Mom, I will leave Baby on his leash from now on." His mother wanted to say, "I told you so," but she bit her lip (which means she did not say it). It was better to have Sam learn the lesson himself. Sam added, "I still like to do things my way, but I'll try to think first before I do something stupid."

His mother tried to hide a smile as she thought, "That's my Sam. He always likes to have his way. And wanting to have your way is not such a bad thing. My Sam is a boy with a real backbone and lots of courage." Sam and Baby, of course, sat down to watch TV in Sam's bedroom. Sam held the leash firmly in his hand, and Baby purred to his heart's content.

THE BOTTOM LINE: Keep your lion on a leash!

Treatment Interventions

Lion Drawing Activity

1. Therapist asks the children what the story means. If they do not "get it," therapist explains that the lion is like out-of-control, unleashed anger. (For teens or adults, it may also represent out-of-control behaviors such as drinking, eating, shopping, porn, texting, gambling, Internet use, etc.)
2. Therapist asks each person to draw a picture of his or her "lion." Discuss each person's lion.
3. Family members share what they do to "leash" their own lion.

Leashing Activity

1. Get into pairs, with parents playing lions and the children playing the caretakers. Parents are encouraged to play with their young children by moving around the room pretending to be wild and unleashed.
2. Ground rules—off leash, the "lions" may act bossy, mean, controlling, and demanding but they may not make actual physical contact. Growling and roaring are permitted.
3. Next, have the children put the lions on the leash, and see how the lions respond to the guidance of the leash.

Cool Down the Volcano!

This activity introduces the concepts of anger triggers, anger prevention, and anger regulation for individuals that report a short fuse or quick temper. Therapist discusses that angry feelings are not a problem; it is what someone does when he or she is angry. For example, "letting off steam" is not as bad as erupting and destroying everything in your path.

1. Family members (or group) are instructed to draw a large volcano and discuss what happens when a volcano gets too hot. Therapist and family discuss the damage a volcano causes when it erupts (burning things in its path, requiring evacuation).
2. Therapist asks family members to discuss what they do when they get too hot and what damage is inflicted when they erupt.
3. Therapist asks family members to write or draw things that make them angry (things that get them "hot") deep inside the volcano: for example, being left out, someone making fun of them, failing at something, being criticized, etc.
4. Therapist asks each family member to identify what makes his or her anger more likely to "erupt"—for example, being too tired or grouchy,

being hungry, having a bad day at work or school, being told what to do, being laughed at, being told no, having bad thoughts, having thoughts of things not being fair, etc.

5. Therapist asks members what they do to prevent an explosion when getting angry. Therapist then asks what family members can do to help one another when they are angry.

6. Therapist identifies stages of an volcanic (anger) eruption and asks family members what they can do to calm down at each phase:

   - First phase—the lava/anger starts to get hot and bubbly. How can we cool it down? Ice cools things down. Can we throw in a little ice? What would be ice for each of you?
   - Something happens to make it worse—inside, it gets hotter and pressure rises. (What can we do to keep the heat down or lower the heat?)
   - The angry lava starts to rise up toward the top. (What can we do to send a warning to the village? Can we do something to prevent the explosion?)
   - The words, behavior, and emotion explode over the top. (What can we do to protect the village below? How do we cool back down as quickly as possible?)

7. Build and set off a volcano:

   - First make the "cone" of the baking soda volcano. Mix 6 cups flour, 2 cups salt, 4 tablespoons cooking oil, and 2 cups of water. The resulting mixture should be smooth and firm (more water may be added if needed).
   - Stand the soda bottle in the baking pan and mold the dough around it into a volcano shape. Don't cover the hole or drop dough into it.
   - Fill the bottle most of the way full with warm water and a bit of red food color (can be done before sculpting if you don't take so long that the water gets cold).
   - Add 6 drops of dishwashing detergent to the bottle contents.
   - Add 2 tablespoons baking soda to the liquid.
   - Slowly pour vinegar into the bottle. Watch out—eruption time!

There is a chemical reaction between the baking soda and vinegar. In this reaction, carbon dioxide gas is produced, which is also present in real volcanoes. As the carbon dioxide gas is produced, pressure builds up inside the plastic bottle, until the gas bubbles (thanks to the detergent) out of the "volcano." Adding a bit of yellow food coloring will result in red-orange lava!

Take-It-Home Discussion Questions

Therapist may assign one or more of the following questions for the child to answer and discuss with parent, foster parent, or staff or prior to the next session.

How am I like Sam? How am I like the lion?

How did Sam feel when his mother told him to keep the lion on the leash?

How did Sam feel when the lion almost hurt him and his mother?

How did the lion feel on and off the leash? How is his behavior different on and off the leash?

Was there a time in my life when I let my "lion" off the "leash"? How did I feel?

What are some things that people need to leash or control in their lives? How about me?

What is hardest for me to "leash" (my own lion)?

When am I most tempted to unleash my lion?

POWER AND CONTROL

The story that follows is about an angry tyrant who mistrusts others. He can't tell the difference between friends and enemies, and behaves as if everyone is an enemy. Discussing the story allows families to become more aware of irrational thinking and overuse of protective defenses.

Figuring out who to trust after you have been abused is a very difficult task. One particular client, for whom this story was written, verbally attacked or disregarded almost anyone that came into his world. In meeting people for the first time, he avoided eye contact, refused to carry on conversation, and assumed that they held malevolent intentions. He did not accept feedback during treatment and was suspicious of intentions. He sexualized his therapist and labeled others as "stupid idiots." He threatened to sue and drew faulty conclusions about most social interactions.

The main barrier to success with this client was his negative perceptions of others. Some clients are able to get past their guardedness in time; others may require psychotropic medication. Hopefully, this story will serve as a bridge to discussing these issues.

THE NEARSIGHTED TYRANT

The king of Castle Go-Away was squinting from the top tower of his castle, watching someone approach by foot. He was quite nearsighted, which means he could not see far away. People walking or riding down the path to his kingdom looked like blurry ants to him, and that was a problem, because he could not tell if they were friend or enemy. The king didn't want to let enemies get too close, and by the time anyone got close enough for recognition, it was too late. The king did not want to put himself or his family in danger.

The king's name was Ty Rant. That is because he would rant and rave at anyone that approached his castle. He had just moved to Castle Go-Away after being reassigned from a kingdom 80 miles away, and he was not very happy about the change. And even though he was new to the kingdom, King Ty Rant had very few visitors.

King Ty Rant's castle was a remarkable structure that protected him and his family from harm. He hardly ever went out, and no one could get in. The 20-foot-thick walls of the 10-story fortress were made of rough stone, and there were iron bars at all the windows. There were small peepholes through which you could view approaching individuals and shoot them if you wished. There was a *double* moat of murky dark water around the entire castle. The first moat was filled with man-eating croco-diles and the second with piranha fish with razor sharp teeth. When the drawbridge of the castle was closed, the only way to get to the castle was by moat, and, of course, no one wished to swim across.

By now, you probably understand why King Ty Rant had very few visitors. And on this particular day, as a small blurry ant-like person approached the castle, the king shouted from the tower to one of his knights, "Sir Geoffrey, is that friend or enemy?"

Came the response: "I don't know, Your Highness. I can't tell yet who it is. Shall I let him come a little closer? Shall I ask who goes there?"

"No!" retorted the king. "It is better to be safe than sorry. Shoot him. Not to kill, of course; just wound him to stop him from coming any closer."

And so Sir Geoffrey shot the person in the leg. The person stopped moving and now looked very much like a fallen blurry black ant.

"Now, go check, and tell me if it is friend or enemy," ordered the king.

Sir Geoffrey ran across the drawbridge and down the path about 100 yards to check on the fallen person, who indeed turned out to be the castle baker—the baker was bringing them their week's supply of bread and pastries.

"Your Highness!" shouted Geoffrey to the king as he dragged the baker back to the castle. "This person is a friend, the castle baker. What shall I do with him?"

"Put him to bed in the castle hospital," replied King Ty Rant. "Better to be safe than sorry!"

They put the baker to bed in the castle hospital, but it would be a long while before any more bread or pastries came their way. The townspeople were very upset with the king for shooting the town baker, since they dearly loved his cinnamon rolls, and now they would have none until he recovered from his gunshot wound.

And so it continued, with the list of those being shot ever growing in length. After a month of "Who goes there?" and "I can't tell," it was Friends 11, Enemies 1. The list of friends was as follows:

Son's math tutor
Castle wine steward
Chief cook
Local priest
Town blacksmith
Daughter's nanny
Head housekeeper
Stable boy
Town tailor
Next-door neighbor
King's mother-in-law

"Oh dear," said Sir Geoffrey with a frown as he discovered their next-door neighbor fallen on the path to the castle. The neighbor clutched an invitation for the king to an upcoming dinner and ball in his hand, but it was clear that he would be doing no dancing (he had been shot in the foot) or entertaining for a long time to come. Sir Geoffrey moved him to the castle hospital with the others.

And when Sir Geoffrey discovered the king's mother-in-law on the path, shot in the arm, he groaned loudly and said out loud to himself in a worried voice, "Your Highness, you are in deep doo-doo now for sure!" Sir Geoffrey then carried the poor woman to the castle hospital and let the queen know she might want to visit her mother in the hospital as soon as possible. He bought a "Get Well Soon" card and flowers for the king to send his mother-in-law but advised him to stay *away* from the hospital for a few days.

That night, Sir Geoffrey approached the rooms of King Ty Rant. "Knock, knock, knock," went Sir Geoffrey's fist on the thick wooden door.

"Who is it?" asked the king

"Geoffrey, Your Highness" came the response.

"Come in," said the king.

"Your Highness," said Geoffrey, "This week we shall have no bread; your son shall have no school; there will be no church services; there will be only cold sandwiches for dinner with no wine; your daughter will be unsupervised; and the horses will need someone to groom them. Your neighbor might now be your enemy, and your mother-in-law may take your wife and move to another kingdom. All these people, as you remember, were shot this week and they are now residing in the castle hospital. I wonder if you might entertain a suggestion, sir?"

The king scowled and rubbed his chin, thoughtfully. "All right, Geoffrey," he replied. "What do you suggest?"

"I suggest, sir, that you do whatever you need to do to *sharpen your focus* when someone is approaching the castle, so that you can tell who is friend and who is foe."

"What do I do to sharpen my focus?" asked the King.

"You'll have to let people get a little closer and then, when they no longer look like ants, you will have clues to tell you which is which," said Geoffrey.

"What clues will help me tell the difference between friends and enemies," King Ty Rant questioned with doubt in his voice. "I don't think anyone can *really* tell the difference!"

Sir Geoffrey answered, "When a friend or relative comes near, he or she is likely to be smiling, laughing, waving, calling out a friendly greeting, or looking you in the eye with recognition. An enemy is more likely to be hiding behind the trees, staying off the path, or using camouflage. Once you sharpen your focus, you will be able to pick out friends (and relatives) from enemies at least 95 out of 100 tries!"

"Tell me why I should bother to sharpen my focus, Geoffrey," asked the king, since he was still not sure he wanted to do this. "I still think it's better to be safe than sorry."

As you can tell, the king could be very stubborn at times . . .

Geoffrey remained patient as he explained, "Well, sir, in the short run, shooting *everyone* keeps you safe. But you lose more than you gain in shooting enemies **and** friends. And in the long run, friends have added value. With a sharper focus, you will be a better leader and have more allies. With more allies, the kingdom has better overall protection. And if an enemy ever gets as close as the moat, there are always the crocodiles and piranha fish to keep you and your family safe."

The king agreed that shooting his mother-in-law and the castle friends over the past week had certainly caused a number of problems.

"OK, Geoffrey," said the king, "I'll do what I need to do to sharpen my focus."

The king kept his word and began letting others come closer on the path so that he could look for clues to identify friends and enemies. The king missed clues and ordered Geoffrey to shoot a friend every once in a while, but for the most part he had learned to tell the difference. King Ty Rant was still a tyrant, but by sharpening his focus, he now had fresh bread, good wine, and allies to help him in times of distress.

THE BOTTOM LINE: Sharpen your focus!

Treatment Interventions

Focusing Activity

1. Therapist brings in binoculars to illustrate types of *focus*.
2. Therapist selects an object in the room and says to the child, "That thing is six feet tall. It's not really two feet tall." When the child corrects the therapist, therapist hands the child the binoculars and asks the child to look through the magnifying side. Point out to the child how much bigger the object looks.
3. Therapist passes around the binoculars and asks each person to look through the magnifying side. Therapist explains that people magnify some negative things such as weaknesses, dangers, mistakes, life events, and failures.
4. Ask members what negative things they magnify in their lives.
5. Therapist suggests that participants need to consciously magnify positive things in themselves and their lives.
6. Pass around the binoculars—while each person holds them and looks through the magnifying side, ask participants what things they need to magnify that are positive.
7. Next, select the same object and say, "That thing is not really two feet tall. It's really six inches tall." When the child corrects the therapist, therapist gives the child the binoculars and asks child to look through the minimizing side. Point out how much smaller the object looks.
8. Therapist passes around the binoculars again and asks each person to look through the minimizing side. Therapist explains that people minimize some positive things such as strengths or successes; they may also minimize negative behaviors toward others.
9. Ask members what sorts of things they minimize.
10. Therapist suggests that family members use their eyes to magnify one another's strengths and life's positive events.
11. Therapist suggests that family members use their eyes to minimize one another's weaknesses or minor disappointments and find ways to overlook them. They also can minimize mistakes or shortcomings in themselves.
12. Pass around the binoculars—each person holds them and says something they want to work at minimizing.
13. For family members who often distort reality or dissociate, therapist may suggest that they check out their perceptions before assuming they are accurate or the "whole picture."

Take-It-Home Discussion Questions

Therapist may assign one or more of the following questions for the child to answer and discuss with parent, foster parent, or staff or prior to the next session.

What would I say to the king to help him make/keep friends?
How can I tell the difference between friends and enemies?
How do I need to sharpen my focus?
How am I out of focus?
What do I need to magnify in myself? In my life?
What do I need to minimize in myself? In my life?
How can I tell who to trust?
Do I ever treat potential friends like enemies?

4

Reducing Hyperactivity
and Agitation

Many child victims of abuse and neglect display hyperactive behavior and impulse-control difficulties, which are also symptoms of ADHD (impulsive type). Traumatized children have grown up in disorganized, inconsistent, and chaotic environments, which leads to attachment difficulties and poor affect modulation. Therapies focused on self-control, relaxation, safety, and arousal reduction help agitated individuals "calm down" and develop better executive functioning so that they become able to think before they act.

The arousal and hyperactivity of traumatized children are subtly different than those seen in the *typical* ADHD child. Typical ADHD children are hyperactive and impulsive but not hyper-vigilant; in fact, they tend to be rather inattentive to cues in the environment. Traumatized children scan their environments carefully and are sensitized to react to perceived environmental threats. Their impulsive and hyperactive behaviors are exacerbated by angry parental outbursts or threats of parental abandonment. They become over-active in response to high levels of physiological arousal.

It is important to evaluate other factors that may contribute to neurological problems and symptoms of hyperactivity and agitation: pre-natal trauma (including intra-uterine exposure to drugs or alcohol, maternal stress), labor and birth complications, exposure to toxins such as lead, streptococcus infections in the first two years of life, and methamphetamine use in the home.

Traumatized children often experience sensory overload. Due to cognitive rigidity, they have difficulty transitioning from one activity to another. They may be easily aroused by sensory input such as noise, crowds, and visual stimulation. Fans, white noise, or sound machines with background sounds of water, wind chimes, ocean, and nature may help restless, vigilant children settle down by inducing relaxation.

Traumatized children may play well alone but become hyperactive in groups due to poor self-regulation. They may also become more agitated in unstructured settings. Some have trouble going to or from school on the bus; moving in the hallways at school; sitting in the lunchroom; and going out to eat. Modifications in the school setting are quite helpful.

Working with these children in family or group settings is very difficult, as their poor impulse control, high arousal, and hyperactivity are disruptive to the therapy process. Some children may be unable to focus in or benefit from therapy until their arousal is managed by psychotropic medication. Therapies focused on self-control, executive functioning, relaxation, and safety plans are helpful in decreasing arousal and reducing sensory overload. The treatment interventions in this chapter are focused on arousal reduction and increasing the relaxation response.

TREATMENT INTERVENTIONS

The Turtle Technique

The turtle technique, a procedure for helping emotionally disturbed children (pre-school through school-age) control their impulsive and aggressive behavior, has been used since the 1970s. Research in this technique indicates that it leads to a decrease in aggressive behavior in both classroom and home.

Schneider and Robin developed this particular self-control technique and were the first to demonstrate its effectiveness for young aggressive students with conduct disorders (Schneider 1974; Robin, Schneider, & Dolnick 1976). The technique consists of four simple components: the "turtle response" (initiated by child or adult), relaxation, problem solving, and peer support.

1. *The Turtle Response.* The technique makes use of the turtle response of withdrawing into a shell or protective space when provoked by the external environment (Fleming, Ritchie, & Fleming 1983). According to Robin et al. (1976), young children may be taught to withdraw into their shell by placing their heads down, locking their arms over their heads, and closing their eyes. They are told that this is how the turtle protects himself/herself and draws strength to face the outside world.

Using a short story and modeling, therapists or staff may teach children to be turtles (or other quiet animals of their choosing—one child always picks a giraffe), soliciting child input throughout.

Once there was a young turtle that got in trouble a lot. He had a bad temper. He was very hyper and did not listen very well. He spent lots of time in time-out!

He got mad when people said things to him. He hit or bit people when he was upset. His friends got upset with him and didn't want to play with him. One day a wise old turtle saw the young turtle getting upset. He said, "You have just what you need to calm down."

Therapist asks, "Do you know what that is?" (Pause and let the children guess.) "That's right, he has his very own shell right on his back."

His older friend said, "All you have to do to calm down is 'do turtle.' I'll count to 3, and when I say 3, I'll say, 'Do turtle.' Let's see how fast you can stop moving and go inside your shell. 1-2-3, 'do turtle.'"

Well, Turtle went inside his shell right away when he heard, '3.' His friend said, "Good job!" The young turtle was now all inside his shell.

Therapist asks children: "What's it like in there for the turtle? Is it dark or light? Is it quiet or noisy? Is he calm or upset? Is he hyper or still? Does he breathe slow and deep; or does he pant like a dog? That's right! Good job!"

The little turtle liked it inside his shell. It was nice and quiet in the dark. He stayed very still and breathed slow and deep. He got rid of all his anger and hyperness. He was really calm!

Therapist asks children: "Do you think we could pretend to be turtles? How would we do that? How would we have a shell? That's right—we can do this (therapist can put head in lap with arms curving up overhead) or this (drop to the floor and crouch)."

Therapist continues: "Let's see how fast we can 'do turtle' when I count 1-2-3 and say, "Do turtle." OK, let's try it. 1-2-3—do turtle—(wait for response). Good job! What's it like inside your shell? Is it dark or light? Is it quiet or noisy? Are you calm or upset? Are you breathing slow and deep or panting? Are you hyper or still?"

Therapist then makes a game out of it, letting the children know it is a game to see who can "do turtle" on command, for the rest of the session. Coach the parents if they are there to also practice giving the command. Praise the children for becoming still, quiet, eyes closed, etc. Within a few tries, the children will drop on command and become quickly silent.

Children may be encouraged to "do turtle" on their own when they get "too hyper," or feel rage or anger, and adults (staff, parents, teachers, therapist) may request that students "do turtle."

2. *Relaxation*. While in the "turtle shell," the children may be taught to relax their muscles and encouraged to take deep breaths in order to cope with emotional tensions.

3. *Problem Solving*. After a period of relaxation, the children are encouraged to come out of their shells to begin a series of problem-solving tactics that allow them to reflect on their behavior (Robin et al. 1976). In the study by Fleming et al. (1983), four basic problem-solving steps were taught to the students: (1) identify the problem, (2) generate alternative solutions,

(3) evaluate alternatives and select the most appropriate, and (4) implement the selected alternative. Both group and individual applications of these steps should be practiced during the learning phase while students are beginning to use the turtle idea.

4. *Peer and Family Support.* This technique has been shown to be effective up through middle school. It is critical that the other members of the family or group respect the child's choice to become a "turtle" for a few moments. The family/group must be instructed to not talk to, joke with, or talk about the child who has chosen to withdraw into his/her shell. Support from others, in the form of ignoring the student during his/her withdrawal, can make this technique very effective.

Up, Up, and Away: Guided Imagery for Stress Reduction

Guided imagery with relaxation is very helpful in decreasing arousal. The therapist creates a relaxing, safe place for the child using a beanbag chair, large floor pillow, recliner, or rocking chair to facilitate relaxation. Giving the child a stuffed animal and soft blanket establishes an atmosphere of safety and comfort.

Once the mood is set (may also want to use sound machine), the therapist invites the child to join him/her in a *safe and relaxing place* to which the child may retreat when needed. The therapist may wish to teach the child how to breathe deeply from the diaphragm with the help of a drinking straw.

1. The therapist encourages the client to breathe slowly and deeply.
2. Therapist asks client to imagine he or she is holding a "bouquet" of five helium balloons outdoors in a safe, relaxing place. Therapist asks the child to describe the place he or she is and what colors the balloons are.
3. Ask the client to tug on the strings and feel the pull.
4. Ask the client to notice the vibrant colors, each one different.
5. Suggest that each different colored balloon holds part of the client's total stress that day.
6. Encourage the client to tug and feel the balloons again, noticing that they can lift up and pull the arm toward the sky.
7. Let client know he/she will be cued to release one balloon at a time, to let the client's stress lift up into the sky.
8. Prompt the release of the first balloon and suggest the client take a deep breath as he/she releases the balloon. Note for the child how easily it moves up and away.
9. With the first balloon, remind client to note the color and follow the balloon with his/her eyes as it lifts up into the sky.

10. Suggest the client track the balloon above the trees and up into the clouds and to watch it closely until the pinprick of color is just visible and then finally disappears.
11. Have client take a deep breath and suggest the client may realize that some of the stress is gone.
12. Last, tell client to let go of one balloon at a time at his or her own pace; to take a deep breath when each balloon finally disappears from sight; and then signal with one finger on one hand when they are all gone. Re-orient the client to the room. Discuss the sensation of letting go.

Darcie's Dots

This technique may be used during individual, group, or family sessions (or at home) in order to help the child (pre-school and elementary age) pay closer attention to his or her behavior. Requires two washable markers.

1. Therapist tells the children the goal is to get more *purple* (any color is fine, and the child may select the color) than black dots.
2. When a child exhibits desirable behavior, the therapist, without much ado, says, "I want to give you a purple dot for X" and puts a dot on the child's hand. The therapist may comment on the appropriate behavior: "I like it when you do X!"
3. When a child exhibits undesirable behavior, the therapist says, "I need to give you a black dot for X" and puts a black dot on the other hand (a warning may be given prior to the black dot, especially for younger children). If the child resists the black dot or runs away, the therapist puts it on a piece of paper.
4. Therapist can also give purple dots to someone who notices or praises someone else's *good* behavior; and a child can avoid a black dot if she/he self-corrects after realizing that a black dot behavior has been displayed. Older children may be allowed to mark their own dots on their hands, but therapist should be in control of the marker.
5. Therapist should give children lots of chances to earn *good* dots for kindness, sharing, and pro-social behaviors.
6. At the end of session, the children count their dots. Those with more good than bad dots get a sticker *and* small piece of candy. Those who improve from the prior week but still have more bad dots get a sticker.

5

Flight

Avoidance, Withdrawal, and Dissociation

Some children with ASD/PTSD resemble children with ADHD (inattentive type). They may be referred to mental health providers for poor concentration, short attention span, and "not listening." They tune others out (and become isolated), do not appear to hear (stare off) when others speak to them, have trouble focusing at school, and seem easily distracted. They even *fall asleep* during difficult sessions (trancelike withdrawal or dissociation) to avoid listening to the therapist.

Yet these children are quite different than *typical* ADHD children. Many are hyper-vigilant and notice details about their environment. Some traumatized children regress to younger age states, doing and saying things they don't later remember doing or saying and reverting to baby talk. Adults often accuse dissociative children of "lying."

One little girl reliably curled up *to take a nap* whenever we discussed past abuse, and only a quickly offered piece of chocolate *woke her up*. She showed other signs of dissociation (baby talk, regressed behavior, rapid changes in mood and cognition), and after seven months in therapy she announced, "I have two brains. One is for feeling and one is for thinking. I can put them to sleep. I put the feeling side to sleep when I don't want to feel. I put the thinking side to sleep when I don't want to think."

To avoid thinking or talking about abuse experiences, some children engage in self-absorbed or obsessive activities. They may play alone for long periods of time. Therapy helps these children become more emotionally attuned and to remain *present* in the face of stress.

Some parents of abused children experienced abuse when they were young, and they may miss signs that their children are being abused. They may "tune out" or change the subject when discussing their child's abuse. When their children reach the age they were at the time of their abuse, they are likely to experience increased levels of stress. These parents often select unsafe partners, trust persons that should not be trusted, and don't tune into the warning bells that ring in most parents' heads when something is not quite right. It is as if their "safety radar" malfunctions.

One mother asked, "Have I ever told you that my husband used to disappear in the middle of the night when I was sleeping. I would wake up and he would be gone. Once I found him in my daughter's room. He didn't have a good reason for being there. Do you think something could have been going on?" For years, the mother had missed this warning sign and had even *forgotten* that her husband used to do this.

Therapy helps parents *tune up* their *risk radar* to make it more sensitive. It helps children remain more emotionally and cognitively present in the face of anxiety. The stories and interventions in this chapter help family members address issues they have been avoiding and learn ways to re-engage.

DISSOCIATION

The next story, *The Mouse Who Became Invisible*, was written for a little girl whose primary coping behavior was to hide. She hid in closets, under tables, and under her bed. She slept on the floor under her bed; and she rarely spoke when spoken to. She ran off when threatened and did not know how to express her thoughts or feelings. She became invisible, and her feelings remained unspoken.

This story's metaphor is about dissociation (becoming invisible) and passivity (losing one's voice). This story's main character finds her voice and becomes more visible to others. Withdrawal and silence are common among abuse victims, who need to be empowered to speak up. Finding one's voice again and becoming more assertive are important therapeutic tasks.

THE MOUSE WHO BECAME INVISIBLE

Did you ever wish you could be invisible? If you were invisible, you could stay up late at night, and no one would know. You could play hide and seek better than anyone else. You could hear what people say when they think you aren't around.

Well, there was once a mouse named Dora Mouse that lived in the town of Naught. Dora was usually "as quiet as a mouse." She stayed in her seat during the school day and did her work; but she slouched down if the teacher called on her and never raised her paw to answer questions. Dora had no friends, mostly because no one really noticed her. If you had asked Joe Smith what color Dora's eyes were or how she dressed, Joe would have said, "I don't know who you're talking about." Dora was rather plain looking—with plain brown fur that matched the color of the floor, short whiskers, and a very ordinary tail. Not even the schoolhouse cat noticed her!

For the most part, Dora lived a life of painful silence. At home, she had learned to be quiet and to stay out of the way, especially when her parents were fighting. Their loud squeaking and biting scared Dora. When she got scared, Dora just hid somewhere with her tail between her legs. Her parents often told her that she was a "good for nothing" mouse. Dora wished that someone could see she was hurting inside, but she was too afraid to tell anyone.

One morning in October, Dora Mouse went to look in the mirror to check her fur before school and noticed an amazing thing. She had started to fade from view.

"My goodness," she said, "my fur looks lighter than it did before and fuzzy around the edges!" Her body sort of blended in with the room. Dora was becoming invisible, but she wasn't really surprised that this was happening.

The silence and pain in her life were erasing her, like an eraser makes colors vanish on a dry erase board. You know how it is—first the colors smear, and as you rub a little harder, the colors blend in with the board. As you keep rubbing, the colors disappear. Soon the board is white again, and you would not even know that there had been writing or drawings on it. That's what silence and pain had done to Dora Mouse.

That day at school, Dora could tell she was nearly invisible. The teacher and other children looked right through her. When she went home that afternoon, Dora ran to look in the mirror again. She could hardly see herself, and as Dora tried to squeak in amazement, no sound came out—her voice was gone, too! That night Dora went to bed early, because Dora was very tired—becoming invisible takes a lot of energy.

In the middle of the night, Dora heard a small noise, and when she opened her eyes, at first she could not tell if she was dreaming or awake.

She saw a funny-looking creature and knew at once that it was an angel. I'm not sure how Dora could tell it was an angel, because the creature had pink hair and was wearing Rollerblades, black leggings, and a leotard. Maybe it was the large purple wings that gave her away!

The angel was smiling and said, "Dora, please don't be afraid."

"Who are you?" asked Dora.

"I'm your *angelic trainer*," replied the creature. "I've come to help you."

"What is an angelic trainer?" asked Dora Mouse.

The trainer replied, "Some people have athletic trainers to help them exercise their bodies. Angelic trainers help people exercise their confidence."

"What do you mean?" asked Dora.

The trainer continued, "If you agree to work with me, I will help you *become visible again and learn to use your voice.*"

"Well," said Dora, "I would like to be visible, and I do want my voice back."

They agreed to work together and shook hands. The trainer's touch was safe, warm, and gentle, not like the touches Dora had at home.

"Where do we start?" asked Dora.

The trainer replied, "Let's start with getting your voice back. You need your voice to be visible."

"But I can't squeak anymore!" said Dora.

The trainer reassured, "Your voice is out of practice. You need more practice."

"First," said the trainer, "let's power breathe! Put your hand in the middle of your belly right under your ribs. When you breathe correctly, your hand will move up and down." Dora put her hand under her ribs, and with each deep breath, she felt her hand rise and fall.

"Good," said the trainer, "Now repeat after me. La, la, la, la, la! SQUEEEEAK!"

"La, la, la, la, la. Squeak," went Dora in a tiny little voice.

Dora's little brown feet and paws became visible.

"Yes," said the trainer, "that's a good start. Now try again."

"La, la, la, la, la! SQUEAK!" went Dora in a louder voice.

Now you could see Dora's eyes, ears, and whiskers.

"What a nice voice you have!" said the trainer.

And finally, in Dora's loudest voice of all: "LA, LA, LA, LA, LA! SQUEAAAAK!!" With each "la," Dora became more clearly defined.

The trainer clapped her hands and cheered, "Hip, hip, hooray!" She said, "Dora, you are already much more visible. Please keep using your voice, every chance you get. Don't be afraid to tell others how you are hurting inside."

Then, *Poof!* The angelic trainer disappeared. Dora sighed deeply and fell into a very deep sleep. She slept soundly until the morning light began to shine into her bedroom window.

When Dora woke up, she felt different. She remembered meeting the angelic trainer and getting her voice back. Dora took a deep breath and gave a small, "Squeak!" Then louder, "SQUEAK!" Then "SQUEAK, SQUEAK, SQUEAK!!!" Dora ran to look in the mirror—there was a clear, visible change in her appearance. She felt more confident than she had in a long time. "La, la, la, la, la! SQUEAK, SQUEAK, SQUEAK!" she sang as she hurried off to school.

Dora gave a small "squeak" as she entered her classroom that day. The teacher looked at her with a smile and said, "Good morning, Dora." A boy mouse heard Dora squeak and smiled at her as she took her seat. She smiled shyly back. Finding her voice and learning how to use it was the key. Dora knew that even though she could not change some things about her life, she no longer had to hide in painful silence.

THE BOTTOM LINE: To become visible, learn to speak (squeak?) up!

Treatment Interventions

Speak (Squeak) Up! (Family or Group)

1. Therapist asks each person for an example of a time he/she did not speak up about something important. What was it that caused each person to lose his or her voice (not speak up on his/her own behalf)?
2. Therapist and members practice vocalizing to get their voices back.
3. Members and therapist can warm up by singing like Dora ("La, la, la, la, la, squeak!")
4. Therapist brings out a puppet and the puppet tells the group or family that she has not had the courage to say something that is bothering her.
5. The therapist asks the members why the puppet might be afraid to say what is on her mind. Discuss.
6. The puppet now tells the group/family what it is he or she was afraid to talk about.
7. Therapist asks the group/family members to give feedback to the puppet about why it is OK to speak up, and to praise the puppet for having the courage to tell them.
8. The puppet now asks the family/group if others keep secrets or have trouble telling others about things that happen. Puppet asks for a show of hands.
9. Each person writes down something he or she has wanted to say to someone else but didn't have the confidence or was afraid to do so.
10. Therapist lets the members know that they will go around, starting with the puppet, and whisper to the person next to them something that is hard to talk about. The person next to them is to praise them and encourage them or give feedback.
11. The puppet now turns to the person next to the therapist and, in a whisper, says something that bothers her, and why she is afraid to talk about it.
12. Therapist asks that person to respond to the puppet.
13. Therapist asks the person to do the same thing—to speak in a whisper to the next person, sharing something that is hard to talk about. And so on.
14. Therapist asks the members how they feel now that they have shared something with the person next to them.
15. Therapist asks members to go around the room again, using a louder and firmer voice, but not shouting, to say what it is that was bothering them.
16. Do this several more times, each time getting louder and firmer, and ending with everyone speaking at once in a good strong voice (but not shouting).

17. Prompt or coach as needed.
18. Ask members if the loudness/firmness of their voices changed anything about their feelings.

Take-It-Home Discussion Questions

Therapist may assign one or more of the following questions for the child to answer and discuss with parent, foster parent, or staff or prior to the next session.

How am I like Dora? How is my life like Dora's life?
When is my pain "invisible" to others?
What things do my parents do that hurt my feelings?
Have I ever felt "invisible"? When?
Have I ever felt "good for nothing"?
Was there ever a time I "lost" my "voice"? What did I do to "get it back"?
How do I feel when I read about Dora Mouse being erased by pain and silence?

AVOIDANCE AND DENIAL

The ostrich in the story that follows puts his head in a hole and ignores dangerous signals. The story addresses the tendency of some parents and children to *look the other way* when risk signs are present and to avoid talking about certain subjects.

Abuse victims and their parents avoid discussing things that make them feel fear, shame, anxiety, and sadness, particularly the abuse itself. Parents and foster parents of children that have been abused often say that the events are in the past and that the *child is over them.* They have the mistaken view that if you provide enough love and protect the child from further abuse, the memories and symptoms will just go away.

Parents may avoid talking about themselves due to feelings of shame, resignation, or sadness. A mother may refuse to talk about past domestic violence but pick one abusive partner after another. Children avoid confronting their parents for fear of losing their love or *causing* still another family rupture.

This story encourages families to begin talking about the things they don't talk about, and, as they do, they improve communication and lower the risk of relapse. For most families, the story's metaphor rings true: "What you don't see can hurt you!"

THE HIDEY HOLE

Ozzie Ostrich loved to walk and play outside, like most other ostriches his age. He really loved going across the street, climbing the small hill up to the train tracks, and then standing on the tracks. He could see for miles ahead and miles back when he stood right in the middle of the tracks on top of that small hill. He felt like king of the hill!

Now, of course, Ozzie's mother had told him over and over, "NEVER stand on the railroad tracks. They are dangerous and you could get hurt." He did not mean to disobey his mother, but it was a hard decision to make—whether to obey his mother or whether to feel like king of the hill on the railroad tracks.

Ozzie knew that trains were dangerous, but he always jumped off the tracks before the train got too close. As he stood on the tracks, he could hear the train whistle.

First, far off in the distance. "Whoo—whoo!" The whistle got louder and louder as the train got closer. *"Whoo—whoo!"* Ozzie felt the tracks rumbling through his tennis shoes, and the train got even closer. "WHOO—WHOO!" He knew it was time to jump when he saw the wheels turning.

One day Ozzie was walking along the tracks and saw a deep hole right in the middle of the tracks. He thought, "You know, I think my head would fit inside that hole!" So Ozzie stuck his head down inside the hole—it was a good fit. It was dark, quiet, and peaceful.

"Wow," he thought, "I like it inside the hole. It's quiet, and I can forget about my problems."

Ozzie started going to the tracks every day. Sometimes, he played king of the hill on the tracks; and when he had a bad day, he stuck his head inside the hole for some peace and quiet.

A couple of days later, Ozzie had a really bad day. He had an argument with his best friend Fred, and he got a bad grade on the spelling test. After school, Ozzie wanted to get away from it all. He ran over to the train tracks as fast as he could.

Ozzie ran up onto the tracks and stood in front of his favorite hole. Before he stuck his head in the hole, the young ostrich looked down the tracks to check for trains. Unfortunately, a train was coming. It was still far off in the distance, perhaps a couple of miles away, and it seemed to be moving slowly. Ozzie could faintly hear the whistle blowing. "Whoo—whoo!"

He thought, "I still have time to put my head in the hole, just for a minute."

So Ozzie put his head in the hole. It was dark, quiet, and cozy. He breathed a sigh of relief. He couldn't hear the train whistle from inside the hole, so Ozzie decided to pretend that the train wasn't coming.

Ozzie thought, "Can't see the train—the train's not coming! Can't hear the train—the train's not coming!" He said this over and over again. He said it so much that he started to believe it!

And when the tracks began to rumble and the train began to approach, Ozzie did not get off the tracks.

His friend Fred had come over to "make up" after the argument at school and saw Ozzie standing on the tracks. Fred saw the train getting closer and closer. Fred hollered, "Ozzie! Get off the tracks!" Of course Ozzie's head was inside the hole and he did not hear Fred hollering at him.

Fred knew he had to do something fast or Ozzie was going to get hit by the train. Fred dashed across the street and ran up to the tracks. He pulled Ozzie's head out of the hole and yanked him off the tracks right before the train zoomed past. Ozzie felt the wind blow his feathers and heard the train's "Whoo-whooooooooo!" as it whizzed by.

Ozzie and Fred were red in the face and panting. Their hearts were pounding! Ozzie realized he had nearly been killed. He said, "Whew! That was a close call! I'm never going to do THAT again."

"Exactly what were you doing?" asked Fred.

Ozzie replied, "I couldn't see or hear the train, so I pretended it wasn't coming."

His friend Fred exclaimed, "That was the stupidest thing I've ever seen! You're just lucky I happened to come by!" Fred added, "You need to keep your head above ground and your eyes wide open to see what's coming!"

Ozzie thanked his friend over and over, and the two of them went to play in the park.

Later that day, Ozzie had a "guilt attack" and told his mother what he had done and what had happened. His mother grounded him to the house for a week. "I want to be able to trust you and know you're safe," she said.

"I know, Mom," said Ozzie. "I'll keep my head above ground from now on!"

THE BOTTOM LINE: What you don't see can hurt you.

Treatment Interventions

Buried Secrets

1. Use a sand tray for the activity.
2. Therapist asks each person to anonymously write two to three things that are hard to talk about; and two to three things that the family avoids talking about. Put the papers inside used medicine containers or plastic eggs and bury them in the sand.
3. Therapist asks family members to dig up one buried container at a time and make a family list of things that are hard to talk about.
4. Therapist processes with the family what types of things are hard to talk about and why they avoid those subjects.
5. Family members identify what would make it easier to talk about the "tough topics."

Family Mural: Heads in the Holes

1. Therapist asks family members to draw a long railroad track on a piece of mural paper or on a large dry erase board.
2. Family members are asked to draw or cut out and paste a large hole for each family member's head on the track and label it with that family member's name.
3. Each family member goes to his or her hole and writes or draws the two main things that the person finds hardest to talk about, avoids the most, or gets the most upset about when discussed.
4. Therapist invites the family to discuss their mural. Look for common themes and provide feedback.
5. Lastly, therapist asks family members what do they need to take their heads out of the holes, i.e., what would make it easier for them to discuss and face these issues.
6. Take a photo of the finished product, especially if on a dry erase board.

Take-It-Home Discussion Questions

Therapist may assign one or more of the following questions for the child to answer and discuss with parent, foster parent, or staff or prior to the next session.

When did I do something dangerous? Did I see the risk?
The ostrich put his head in a hole when he was stressed. How do I cope with stress?
What are some other things I could do to handle stress?

How am I like the ostrich? When am I most likely to put my head in the hole?

What can I do to keep my head above ground and my eyes wide open?

What topics does our family avoid talking about the most?

Have I ever pretended that the "train" wasn't coming (missed a warning sign that something was wrong, perhaps in my health, in a relationship, with my children, or at a job)?

DEPERSONALIZATION

Some individuals *freeze* or become numb following abuse, cutting off their emotions, withdrawing trust, and isolating and/or disengaging from those around them. Many abused children have difficulty developing trust and attachment due their avoidant style of relating to others.

In the next story, an iceberg travels to a warmer climate and thaws in order to experience a new kind of life. The story's metaphor is about taking a risk and allowing oneself to experience change. The image of an iceberg seeds the idea that aspects of the person may be *out of view* below the surface.

The story was written for work with a memorable little ten-year-old boy who had *frozen* his feelings. He was like a little robot, with overly controlled affect and the inability to engage in spontaneous play. He compulsively painted his hands different colors during group therapy and was quite sexualized. He had never really been a child, and his parents had introduced him to the *birds and the bees* through pornography.

This story provided a metaphor that helped this overly adult ten-year-old become more of a child as we focused on attachment development, emotional expression, and trust. The story leads nicely into therapy activities that address these issues.

TIME FOR A THAW

Once upon a time, there was an iceberg that lived near the North Pole. He was frozen solid, hard as a rock, and very cold. Polar bears and Arctic foxes walked on him, and his only other companions were the whales in the ocean.

Like most icebergs, he had a huge secret hidden part of him that remained below the surface of the water. Ships stayed far away, for fear of running aground on his hidden depths.

One day a bird flew down out of the clouds and landed on him. The bird shivered and said, "It's too cold up here. Time for me to fly back down south."

"Please don't leave," said the iceberg. "You just got here! Tell me about the other places you have been and all the things you've seen. Where is *down south*?" Life was pretty lonely for the iceberg, since hardly anyone came to the North Pole.

"It is like another world," said the bird. "It is a place where there are no icebergs. The water never freezes completely, and lots of people come to visit. There are sandy places called beaches, and there are seals and dolphins and all sorts of fish and birds." The bird talked about beautiful places called Maine, North Carolina, and Daytona Beach, Florida.

The iceberg asked, "Do you think I would like it *down south*? Could I go live there? I might be ready for a change."

"Well, you could," said the bird, "but it would be a big change. You would never be an iceberg again. Your ice would melt and you would turn into warmer ocean water. Your water would be transparent, and you would have nothing to hide."

The iceberg said, "Change is not a bad thing. I can't imagine a world like the one you just described—I have lived frozen at the North Pole my whole life. Perhaps I would like it, but I don't know how to get there. Would you show me the way?"

"It's a long journey," said the bird. "And even longer if I have to fly by way of the ocean coast. I guess I can take the long way around the coast and let you follow, since I'm heading south anyway."

And so the bird led the iceberg many, many thousands of miles through the ocean. It was a long and difficult journey. The blinding sleet and snow made it hard to see where they were going, and the icy, blustery wind mocked them. "Go back to where you came from—you will never be able to finish this treacherous journey!"

But the iceberg and bird did not give up. The bird guided his iceberg friend, day and night, and the iceberg moved through the frigid waters.

Finally, they reached warmer waters, and the journey was easier. As the iceberg moved into warmer waters, he started to melt. It felt good. He was no longer frozen solid hard as a rock. He was actually getting a little slushy around the edges. When they got to Maine, it was springtime, and a cold breeze was blowing along the coast. The sun was shining bright, and waters were cold with large waves breaking on the rocky shore.

"I think I'll stop here," the iceberg said to the bird. "It's pleasant, cool, and very beautiful. So I'll bid you adieu." In case you don't know it, "adieu" is a fancy French word for "good-bye." Don't ask me why he didn't just say "good-bye," but perhaps all the traveling had gone to his head! The bird promised to visit on the next trip "up north" and flew off toward Boston and other points south.

As spring passed, the waters warmed in the summer sun, until the iceberg melted completely. He was now part of the bigger ocean. He really liked the warmer climate and all the people that came to look at the ocean waves crashing on the rocks. He wasn't alone like he had been at the North Pole, since there were seals, birds, fish, and dolphins all around. The iceberg enjoyed watching the cute little puffins that settled on the rocks and fished in his waters.

"This place feels like home," he said. "I'm glad I stayed here—it's a good place to belong."

Soon summer passed, and the lovely rich autumn colors painted the trees on the shoreline. Eventually, winter arrived, with frosty air, a layer of hard ice along the rocky banks, and deep snow that lasted until spring.

The iceberg liked his new home in Maine and the changing seasons. He liked spring and summer best, but the icy cold of winter didn't bother him as long as he knew that spring would soon follow. He had found the changes he sought, and by thawing, he had opened himself to a whole new world.

THE BOTTOM LINE: It may be time to make a move.

Treatment Interventions

The Family Berg

1. Therapist asks family members if they know the story of the *Titanic*. Therapist uses the *Titanic* story as an example of how something we do not see can be very dangerous and result in harm if we are not on the lookout and aware of what is below the surface. Therapist reminds members that the *Titanic* was supposed to be unsinkable—those on it overestimated its strengths and ignored its weaknesses.
2. Therapist asks family members to draw an iceberg with a line at the water's surface, part of the ice above the waterline and part below.
3. Therapist asks family members to write or draw things below the surface of the water that they hide from others or avoid talking about. Therapist suggests that family members include, below the surface, weaknesses they have but don't like or things they have done that embarrass or shame them. Discuss.
4. Next, the therapist asks the family to decorate the iceberg above the surface with things that are strengths, hobbies, talents, etc. Discuss.
5. Point out that as they rely on their strengths, family members will find it easier to deal with the things below the surface.

Take-It-Home Discussion Questions

Therapist may assign one or more of the following questions for the child to answer and discuss with parent, foster parent, or staff or prior to the next session.

How am I like the iceberg? Am I more hard or slushy or liquid?
When I am "hard and cold" do I ever get stubborn, isolated, or self-centered?
The iceberg had to make a big change—what did it give up, and what did it gain from the move?
When do I avoid being around others?
What is an area of my life in which I dream of making a radical change?
Is there a chunk of ice inside me that needs to melt?

6

Reducing Worry, Fear, and Anxiety

Aposhyan (2005) is insightful in stating that "fundamental to recovering from trauma is the restoration of the feeling of safety in our bodies" (p. 252). Children that have experienced trauma, especially multiple times, are anxious and fearful, on the lookout for behaviors or circumstances that preceded or accompanied abuse or neglect, i.e., warning signs (cues) that the family might return to their former *bad habits*. Fear and anxiety often result in sleep difficulties, such as bad dreams or trouble getting or staying asleep. Anxious children have difficulty focusing in school.

There is a higher risk of abuse and, subsequently, PTSD for children raised in disorganized and/or unpredictable environments, particularly when there is substance abuse in the home. After the abuse has stopped, traumatized children are sensitized to potential danger. When they see, hear, or feel cues that are perceived as a risk of further harm they may freeze, withdraw, dissociate, regress, become hyperactive, or seek adult comfort.

Examples of things that can raise a child's anxiety following abuse are parental absence, loud voices or cursing, an adult threatening or posturing, hearing someone's footsteps in the hallway, being in a certain room of the house, nighttime, an adult coming into a room and closing a door, or an adult entering the bathroom.

Abused children may develop fears of the dark, of making mistakes, of getting too fat, of being away from home, of getting sick, of the parent dying, or of getting hurt. Some children develop obsessive compulsive rituals or tic-like symptoms. Abused children may fear being around siblings that used to hurt them.

Children need coping mechanisms to cope with fear and anxiety. It is important that they develop self-efficacy and mastery over the feared environment. Young children ages three to six naturally engage in magical thinking, and there are many "magical" interventions that help children manage anxiety. Older children may benefit from the use of coping rituals or guided imagery at times when anxiety is high.

Adults should not minimize children's fears, regardless of age. Some children (and adults) will feel much "younger" at night, if that is when most abuse occurred. They need to be able to decrease fear and physiological arousal while maximizing relaxation. Activities such as yoga, meditation, therapeutic massage, acupuncture, acupressure, self-hypnosis, etc., are quite helpful.

Traumatized individuals benefit from telling their stories over the course of treatment—the purpose of the trauma narrative in TF-CBT is to help children deal with the trauma and feel safe again. When individuals allow themselves to experience (not avoid) anxiety, their high levels of arousal dissipate, and they can develop coping skills and self-efficacy. Many individuals avoid talking about their experiences—after all, who likes to feel fear, shame, panic, or anxiety?

We have found that the trauma narrative may take a variety of formats. Certainly, a trauma story may be in the form of a book. It may also take the form of a comic book, a series of drawings, a puppet show, a play, a dry erase board saga, a sand tray or dollhouse enactment, or a metaphorical story parallel to the child's own that arouses the same affect.

A Bear of a Different Color is a good story to use when working on a child's trauma narrative. By starting with the metaphor and play activities, the child is more easily linked to talking directly about his or her own trauma experience with much less avoidance.

Particularly for cognitively delayed individuals and young children, story-*telling* involves the use of experiential activities that follow *a road less traveled* to a *land* in the right brain where sensory, intuitive, emotional, kinesthetic memories reside. This road allows clients to experientially process what has eluded them and to make meaning of the past.

Metaphor, play, and art are readily available tools that help clients tell their stories in parallel but meaningful ways. Experiential treatment activates emotion and springboards the client toward change.

LETTING GO

The story that follows, *The Burden Bag*, is an endearing tale of a worrying young rabbit. The therapist will need to do little more than read the story with the child, and many children will enjoy having a puppet in hand to act out the drama. The metaphor of the burden-laden backpack is one that any child of school age will relate to easily. People of all ages understand the notion of being heavy with worries and needing to let go.

THE BURDEN BAG

Jack was a young rabbit that moved as slow as a turtle. Jack was not sick or old or physically challenged—he just moved very slowly. His forehead was lined, his eyes drooped, and even when he smiled, Jack Rabbit looked tired and sad.

One sunny day, Jack and a group of his friends were hopping through the meadow. The other rabbits were hopping with lots of energy. "Hippety, hippety hop" they went, but Jack was going "Thud-drag . . . Thud-drag . . ." at a very slow pace.

As the group hopped along, they came across a kindly older rabbit, a good friend of Jack's family. The older friend watched the "hippety hopping" and "hop-thudding" and scratched his head with his large rear foot.

"Jack Rabbit," he said, "you don't run or jump like the other young rabbits. You are moving slower than a turtle in mud!"

The older rabbit then saw that Jack was wearing a large, overstuffed, very heavy backpack. It pulled on Jack's shoulders, sagging halfway down to the ground! There was a label in big red letters on the outside of the backpack, but it wasn't Jack's name. It said, *Jack's Burdens!* Burdens, by the way, are problems that worry you and weigh you down.

Jack's friend said, "Why are you carrying that heavy backpack? You could hop faster if you took it off."

Jack said firmly, "NO—I NEVER take it off."

His older friend asked, "Don't you take it off to eat?"

"No," Jack said, "not to eat."

"What about to sleep?"

"No," he said, "not to sleep."

"Well, surely you take it off to play?"

By this time Jack felt a little impatient and said, "I *TOLD* you I *NEVER* take it off. Not even to play!"

The older rabbit was very curious. He knew it was really none of his business, but he still asked, "What's in it? Is it schoolbooks? Or rocks? It looks so heavy!"

Jack did not mind telling him what was in the backpack and said, "This is my bag of burdens. They *are* heavy!"

The older rabbit was still quite curious and asked, "Can I look inside it? I can't believe a young rabbit like you could have so many burdens."

Jack replied, ""You can look inside if you want." So the wise old rabbit went behind Jack, opened the backpack, and peered down inside. There were many Ziploc bags of burdens in the backpack. Each bag was neatly labeled with colored permanent marker.

The first bag, with a blue label, said, *Stupid Mistakes.* The second bag, with the green label, said, *Rejections.* (Rejection is when someone you like stops liking you back.) A third bag of burdens said, *Family Problems.*

The older rabbit took a peek inside the *Family Problems* bag and remarked, "Many of these family problems have other people's names on them. Why would you carry around someone else's problems?"

"I like to help out," said Jack.

The fourth bag of burdens smelled really AWFUL, and it was labeled in purple: *Imperfections.* The young rabbit explained, "Those are things about me that aren't perfect, like my warts, my big feet, and my crooked teeth."

The wise rabbit said, "No one's perfect. If you want to jump like other rabbits, you need to get rid of these burdens. A rabbit is not meant to move as slow as a turtle!"

Jack argued with him and cried and pouted. He begged, "I've been collecting these burdens my whole life. Can't I just keep a few? I won't know what to do without them!"

"No," said the older rabbit, "It's time to let them go. You can carry around a few 'daily concerns,' if you like, but not burdens."

Finally, Jack agreed that the backpack was *very* heavy and kept him from enjoying his life. He knew he needed to lighten his load.

His friend said, "Come with me. I know just the place to take your burdens. It's a very special place, through the woods."

"Lead the way," said Jack.

Together they hopped down a rocky path and through the woods.

"Here it is," said Jack's friend, as they stopped before a beautiful lake. "This is a bottomless lake."

Jack said in disbelief, "*NO* bottom?"

"That's right," said his friend as he pointed toward the lake. "Look at the sign over there."

Jack looked where his friend pointed and saw a big sign next to the lake. It read, *NO FISHING ALLOWED.* His friend said, "If you throw something in there it is gone for good."

"Aha," said Jack. "I know what you want me to do. You want me to throw my burdens in that lake." He took a small step back, not sure he was quite ready to do what he needed to do.

"It's OK," said his friend. "You know what you need to do." Jack realized he was ready and nodded his head in agreement.

Jack took the backpack off, and his friend helped him take all the burden bags out. Together they unzipped all the bags. "OK, here we go!" said his friend, as he handed Jack a burden. Jack pulled his arm back as far as he could, took a deep breath, and then threw the burden with all his might. The burden flew out over the water and came down with a big *Plop!* Jack watched as it hit the water and sank below the surface.

Letting go of that first burden gave Jack courage. He threw the burdens out in the middle of the lake, one by one, and watched them sink.

As each burden hit the lake, Jack saw big circles of ripples spreading out on top of the water. As Jack watched the ripples spread out, his heart grew lighter and lighter. Before Jack knew it, he was standing on the edge of the lake with an empty backpack.

Jack had a sudden moment of doubt. "Oh my goodness, what have I done? What will I do with an empty backpack?"

His friend said, "Throw it in too."

Somewhat reluctantly, Jack threw his backpack into the lake and watched it sink. He suddenly felt hopeful and took a quick hop forward.

Jack thanked his friend for helping him and hopped home, his head held high. When he got home, he told his mother about his day, with great excitement.

"I'm proud of you, Jack," said his mother, "for having the courage to throw away your burden collection."

"Mom," said Jack, "I'm a little worried that sooner or later I'll be tempted to collect burdens again." Jack knew that collecting burdens was a bad habit. Everyone knows that it is hard to break a bad habit!

His mother suggested, "What you need is a new backpack!" She went to the rabbit hole closet and came back with a brand new backpack with thick cushioned straps. On the front pocket, it said, *Blessings*.

"What are *Blessings*?" asked Jack.

"Blessings," replied his mother, "are good things, like carrots and lettuce and making new friends. When you notice a blessing during the day, stuff it in this bag. At the end of the day, you can count your blessings."

"I like that idea," said Jack. "But," he added, "what can I do if I have a bad day and start collecting burdens again?"

His mother answered, "If you start to collect burdens again, the lake is always a good backup plan. After all, you're only rabbit."

In case you did not know it, that's rabbit for "You're only human." It's what you say to someone when you want to remind him or her that no one is perfect and everyone makes mistakes. So whether you are "only rabbit" or "only human," you may want to do something to lighten your load. And don't forget to count your blessings!

THE BOTTOM LINE: Lighten your load and count your blessings!

Treatment Interventions

The activities in this section focus on identifying sources of worry and gaining control over cognitions and the accompanying emotions. The story allows individuals to consider all sorts of things that they have been carrying around (guilt, shame, fear, etc.) but wish to leave behind.

No Fishing!

Therapist can purchase dissolvable rice paper at any magic store or online. There is a brand name paper called Dissolvo that is useful for these purposes.

1. The therapist invites family or group members to discuss burdens and how they weigh people down.
2. Therapist provides materials (brown paper bag onto which straps can be stapled, glue, glitter, and markers, twine or ribbon for straps) for family members to use to make and decorate a family burden bag. (In a group, children may make individual backpacks.)
3. Therapist provides each family or group member with two small pieces of Dissolvo paper and asks each to write down two burdens that they have carried around for a long time but wish to let go of.
4. Ask members to share their burdens with one another and discuss why they want to let them go.
5. Therapist asks members to put their burdens in the backpack.
6. Therapist takes members on a walk to a stream or to a restroom.
7. Family members take the burdens out of the backpack and drop them in the water.
8. As the paper dissolves, remind family members that once they let go of their burdens, they can't be retrieved.
9. Ask members to write down and discuss what sorts of blessings they have experienced that day or in the past week.
10. Ask members to re-decorate the burden backpack and fill it with blessings; take them home and look at them every day!

Take-It-Home Discussion Questions

Therapist may assign one or more of the following questions for the child to answer and discuss with parent, foster parent, or staff or prior to the next session.

How am I like Jack?
What do I worry about the most?
What keeps children from telling adults about their worries?

What is a worry that I can't or don't talk about

What advice do I have for Jack?

What are two blessings that happened to me this week?

What are three burdens (problems/worries) I have carried around for a long time?

What burdens do I want to get rid of?

How will I feel when I finally let go of my burdens?

Do I pay more attention to blessings or burdens? How can I pay more attention to blessings?

ANXIETY REDUCTION AND CONTAINMENT

The following story, *Wrap It Up!*, was written for use with any anxious child who is obsessing about or worrying about something to the point that it interferes with sleep or daily functioning. Some children have more difficulty than others in letting go of the memories of abuse. These children process the abuse over and over, but the emotionality of having been abused does not subside. Some of these children start worrying about other areas of their lives that are outside their control. If this type of child experiences further trauma or stress, it may lead to disruption in sleep, appetite, and mood. Anxious, fretful children need interventions that give them an increased sense of control and competence. They need help to contain their anxiety and *Wrap It Up!* does just that.

WRAP IT UP!

Sara Spider was perched in the middle of a large web, a frown on her face and huge wrinkles on her somewhat-hairy brow. Her friend Torrence Tarantula, a large funnel-web spider, approached from the ground below and called up to her.

"Yoo-hoo," he called up to her. "Why are you looking so glum? It's a beautiful Saturday morning and the sun is shining. What more could you want?"

"Torrence," said Sara, "please go away and leave me alone. I'm in a bad mood."

"OK," said Torrence. "I understand. We all have bad moods and need our privacy. But before I go, is there anything I can do to help?"

"I don't know," replied Sara. "I'll tell you what's bothering me, and see what you think."

Sara continued, "Last September, I went through a tough time in my life. Do you remember the bad windstorm that came through Louisville and blew down all the trees and power lines?"

"Sure," said Torrence. "It was a terrible storm. The wind blew at 70 miles per hour. It was like a tornado came through!"

"Yes," agreed Sara. "Well, during the windstorm my web, with all my children in it, blew away. I hid under a rock for months after the storm and was afraid to rebuild my nest."

"How did you handle it?" asked Torrence.

"I went to my spider counselor and talked about it," Sara replied. "My counselor helped me understand that bad things happen sometimes. The counselor reminded me that I have many good things in my life and that I could rebuild my web. I did rebuild my web and even found some of my babies that blew away."

Sara was deep in thought. "I felt better after my counseling sessions, but I haven't been able to get thoughts of the storm out of my head. Sometimes I even dream about it. Whenever the wind blows, I go hide under a rock."

Torrence answered, "Oh, so you are still carrying it around. And you feel out of control, like the memories are with you wherever you go?"

"Yes," said Sara. "That's it exactly!"

Torrence hesitated and then spoke again. "Maybe you have forgotten something."

"What?" asked Sara.

"You have everything you need to wrap up your memories, put them away, and keep them from coming back to bother you."

"What exactly are you talking about?" queried Sara.

Torrence answered, "Once you talk about bad things and understand them, you can put them away. You have web silk any time you need it.

Just like you wrap up an insect that you catch in your web for food, you can catch your bad memories or worries in the web of your mind. After you catch them, you can wrap them up tightly like a cocoon, and put them away where they won't bother you anymore."

He added, "If you do this, you can even keep memories and worries out of your dreams. Just remind yourself each morning and each night to wrap up things that might bother your sleep. After all, you are a worrier, Sara. You may need to work a little harder than most spiders to remind yourself not to worry."

Sara's face lit up as if a light had come on. Her eyes looked brighter as she realized she might have some control over the memories and thoughts that had taken over her mind.

Sara admitted, "Yes, Torrence. I have always been a bit of a worrier. I obsess about many things and can't get them out of my mind. I'll have to try this."

That night as Sara went to bed, she imagined catching the picture of the windstorm in her web. She grinned as she saw it stick to the web and realized she had it just where she wanted it—out of her mind and caught fast. She then imagined herself wrapping up the bad memory in a compact, white cocoon, so tight that nothing could get out. As she spun the thread and the cocoon took shape, Sara took a deep breath and relaxed.

By the time Sara finished wrapping the memory inside the cocoon, she was surprisingly tired. Sara fell asleep and that night, not one bad memory touched her dreams.

The next day, early in the morning, Sara called out for Torrence.

"Yoo-hoo! Torrence! Yoo-hoo!"

Torrence slowly crawled out of his funnel web on the ground and answered, while rubbing sleep out of his eyes, "Hello, Sara. It's very early. How are you today?"

"Much better, Torrence," replied Sara. "I tried what you suggested and got a good night's sleep. From now on, if I obsess about something and can't get it out of my mind, I'll *wrap it up*. Thank you for reminding me that I have what I need to control the things that bother me.

THE BOTTOM LINE: Wrap it up!

Treatment Interventions

Wrap It Up like a Spider

Children's worries, memories, fears, and anxiety sometimes interfere with sleep or lead to bad dreams. This activity helps children develop self-control over intrusive thoughts and feelings.

Duct tape, empty toilet paper roles, and paper towel tubes will be needed for this activity.

1. Therapist tells the child that they will be "playing spider" as they talk about bad memories. The child and the therapist will use the Web Worksheet (see page 95) to "catch" memories of abuse, worries, and fears that bother the child. These may be worries they have during the day or things they dream about at night.
2. Like spiders, they will spin silk and use it to wrap up all the "bad stuff" at the end of the session, like spiders use silk to wrap up insects they catch in their webs.
3. Therapist reminds the child that once the scary thoughts are wrapped up, they won't be able to interfere with dreams or sleep.
4. During the session, if the child gets upset as memories are relayed, the child can be reminded to "catch" them in the web.
5. At the end of the session, therapist directs child to crumple up the paper, stuff it in a tube, and wrap the tube tightly with duct tape.
6. Therapist and child dispose of the tube in the trash.

The Smooth Stone (Anxiety-Reduction Technique)

1. Therapist shows members a smooth stone and tells them they will be passing it around the circle.
2. Therapist tells the group members the steps to use in passing the stone:

   - Hold it firmly and say something you worry about a lot.
   - Say the magic words: "No more worry about X!" OR make up your own magic words.
   - Imagine that you are passing the worry from inside you, down your arm through your hand, into the stone.
   - Take a deep, cleansing breath.
   - Squeeze or touch the stone once and pass it to the next person.

3. Therapist gives the stone to a group member. Talk the first person through the steps and coach the breathing as needed.

WEB WORKSHEET

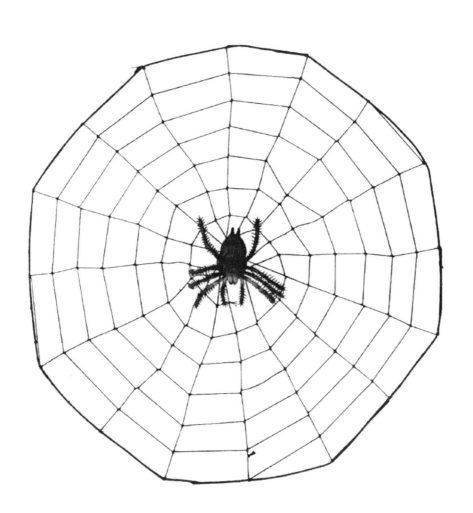

Take-It-Home Discussion Questions

   Therapist may assign one or more of the following questions for the child to answer and discuss with parent, foster parent, or staff or prior to the next session.

   How am I like Sara Spider?
   What do I worry about?
   Do any of my worries sneak into my dreams?
   Do I think about things too much long after they are over?
   Do my worries ever keep me from doing things?
   Do I have worries or fears that keep me from enjoying life?
   What in my life is hardest for me to control or change?
   Does my worrying help me or hurt me? How does that make me feel?

7

Disrupted Attachment

Coping with Loss and Renewing Trust

Children raised in abusive or neglectful homes may develop insecure attachments to their primary caregivers. Disrupted attachment affects many aspects of a child's development. Insecurely attached children experience problems with self-esteem, trust, and mood regulation, in part due to neurobiological changes. Access to nurturing, consistently available secondary attachment relationships is crucial for these children. Therapy needs to address parent-child interaction; and when a child can't return home, group home staff and foster parents must provide caring, individualized attention to ensure the development of secure attachment.

In *The Developing Mind*, Siegel describes the types of relationships that enhance memory, emotion, and self-awareness. Deeply felt emotions have the capacity to change brain functioning and are communicated in facial expressions, eye contact, touch, posture, movements, pace and timing, intensity, and tone of voice. In abusive or neglectful families, these forms of communication are impaired.

Noted researcher Allen N. Schore, in *Affect Regulation and the Origin of the Self* (1994), cites studies that show increased brain development in young children at ages two to three when they are confronted with non-overwhelming challenge and engage in conflict resolution with the help of their caregivers. Segal (n.d.) suggests that, conversely, overwhelming challenge (without resolution) results in infant-caregiver stress and inhibits the growth of brain cells, thus interfering with attachment. Abuse and neglect have a debilitative effect on normative brain development and result in cognitive, emotional, and social deficits.

Joelle Belmonte, on an excellent attachment website, http://www
.jeannesegal.com/eq/relationships_brain_evolution.html, lists a number of

causes of insecure attachment, including physical neglect, emotional neglect, emotional abuse, physical or sexual abuse, separation from primary caregiver, inconsistency of primary caregiver, frequent moves or placements, traumatic experiences, maternal depression, maternal addiction to alcohol or drugs, and being parented by a young, inexperienced mother without parenting skills.

Trauma recovery requires a focus on attachment relationships. Programs that enhance parent-child relationships, such as Bavolek's Nurturing Parenting Program, help strengthen attachment bonds through parent-child activities and psycho-education (www.nurturingparenting.com).

The infant attachment process begins as soon as the child is born, to ensure survival via a strong connection with a protective, nurturing caregiver. Infants signal caregivers for proximity with crying, gaze, and vocalization. Nurturing caregivers feed, cuddle, and hold infants, responding promptly to cries of hunger, pain, or fatigue. Watchful parents learn the different cries of their babies and seek to promptly and consistently meet the needs of their children.

Within a few months after birth, a more social relationship with the caregiver begins to develop, a bi-directional, reciprocal *dance*. The infant smiles, coos, and imitates the caregiver; and the caregiver responds promptly to the infant's signals. Infants are tremendously responsive to the gaze, smell, touch, and facial expressions of their caregivers, *programmed* at birth to respond to the details of a human face. Most parents are equally responsive to their infants.

Through the parent-child social relationship, the capacity for play and socialization develops, and the caregiver-child relationship deepens. There is an excellent description of a process called attunement by trauma expert Bruce Perry at the Scholastic website. "Attunement" writes Perry (2008), "is being aware of, and responsive to, another." Perry describes exquisitely the non-verbal process whereby our brains perceive signals from others through facial expressions, gestures, tone of voice, eye gaze, etc. The brain processes both the words spoken and the non-verbal cues, integrating them so that meaning is derived. Through this process, a child can sense someone's interest, approval, enthusiasm, or lack thereof.

For more detailed information about attachment and caregiver qualities, see *The Infant Caregiver Project*, University of Delaware (http://icp.psych.udel.edu/about.htm).

The capacity for secure attachment develops when a child has consistent, loving responses to his or her needs, especially during the first two years of life.

An insecure attachment is more likely to develop when a child cannot rely on his or her caregiver. In abusive homes, the caregiver is a source of pain and fear, which creates confusion and ambivalence in the infant. The adult who threatens the child's well-being is the same adult the child must turn to for survival and nurturance. The children in abusive homes may display disorganized, resistant, anxious, ambivalent, or avoidant behaviors. In neglectful homes, care is provided inconsistently, if at all, and children are left to take care of themselves.

Children with attachment deficits display many types of behaviors. They may treat adults like "apples in a basket." To them, adults are interchangeable and they all look and act alike. There is little or no emotional investment. Attachment-disordered children may run away or hide from others in closets or behind furniture. They may refuse to come when called and play alone for long hours. They may hoard food, urinate in unusual places, void in their pants, or smear feces.

Some anxiously attached children cling to adults and refuse to separate. Some won't ask for adult help, appearing very controlled or autonomous; and others are dependent on adults in an age-inappropriate way. Some are bossy and demanding, and others do everything they can to please adults. Children who are insecurely attached wander too far from their parents or cling excessively; and their parents either do not monitor them closely enough or overprotect them.

Regardless of attachment type, children experience loss and anxiety when they are separated from their parents during periods of foster care, group home placement, or hospitalization.

Treatment interventions focused on nurturance, trust, and relationship development remediate some of the effects of insecure attachment. Secondary attachments provide the child with a secure base, allowing for neurobiological change and enhancing social and emotional development. But the longer children endure abuse, the harder it becomes for them to trust others later in life.

The interventions in this chapter are designed to enhance adult-child relationships. It takes repeated, long-term nurturing behavior to build trust in children whose needs were disregarded in the past. Children often test caregivers, to see if they care enough to *put up with them* or if they will be rejected again.

ATTACHMENT AND TRUST

The next story, *Run Away Ralph*, is a story with an attachment metaphor. Like many children placed in out-of-home care, Ralph tests those who care for him and sees if they will give up on him when he runs away. Many children placed in out-of-home care run away or threaten to do so, testing their caregivers and seeking to be returned to a secure base. It is a recapitulation of the attachment stage of infancy, when infants venture further and further from their "home base." Attuned parents let their children explore, but not too far away, and they fetch them and bring them back if needed. Through strong, repeated connections, Ralph learns to trust the staff who care for him.

RUN AWAY RALPH

Ralph the Chipmunk attended Happy Hollow Boarding School, a very nice boarding school out in the country. In case you do not know it, a boarding school is a school where the children live AND go to school. They go home on visits sometimes, and their parents may visit them at school, but they spend most of their time at the boarding school.

Run Away Ralph was his nickname, and he got that name honestly. Someone would look the other way, and he would be gone in a flash. "Zoom!" went Ralph. Out the door he went—then down the steps, down the driveway, and across the grassy field to the road. The road was by the railroad tracks, but Ralph never crossed the street. He knew that crossing the street would be a very dangerous thing to do.

You might ask why Ralph ran away so much. Well, Ralph was a little mad at his parents for sending him away to Happy Hollow Boarding School, and he wished he could go back home.

When he was in a bad mood, he thought, "They *only* want me home if I do what they want. They only want me home if I'm perfect. They only want me home if they're in a good mood. Well, I'm not perfect and I'm never going to be! *That's* why they sent me away to boarding school!"

So Ralph had started running away.

When Ralph was in a bad mood, he shouted, "I'm going to run away because you're so mean to me!"

When Ralph was in a sad mood, he cried, "I'm going to run away, because no one loves me!"

If someone corrected Ralph, he shouted, "I'm going to run away, because everyone picks on me!"

And when Ralph was in a good mood, he said (with a smile on his face), "I'm going to run away, and when you find me, you can give me a big hug."

When Ralph ran off, everyone ran after him, because no one wanted him to get lost or hurt. They wished that he could quit running away, but they couldn't figure out how to help Ralph stay in one place.

So one day, they all decided to play hide and go seek. "You get to hide," they told Ralph. "You can be the hider all day. In fact, let's play hide and go seek until you get tired of running and hiding. Whoever finds you gets to give you a high-five, a Hershey Kiss, or a hug, whichever you want."

"I'll never get tired of running and hiding," said Ralph.

"We'll see," said the people at Happy Hollow. "Ready, set, go!" they said as they covered their eyes and counted to 25.

It was 9 AM when they started playing the game. They counted, and Ralph hid. First he hid in the bushes, then behind the sofa, then up the hill by the dog's fence, then down by the creek, then under his bed, then in a closet, then out under the picnic table, then in his clothes closet. Each time Ralph hid, the Happy Hollow staff found him.

By noon, Ralph had 8 Hershey Kisses, 7 bear hugs, and 10 high-fives. He was also running out of places to hide, so Ralph decided to go a little further away. He hid down the road, across the grassy field, behind the swing set, and out in the trash area. Each time Ralph hid, they found him.

Ralph was getting a little tired by 2 PM. By now he had 15 Hershey Kisses, 10 big bear hugs, and 15 high-fives. He was really having trouble thinking of safe new places to hide. So Ralph started repeating the hiding places.

By 6 PM Ralph was very tired. He wanted to stop playing hide and go seek to eat dinner, but he didn't want to admit he had run out of steam. So he kept playing and missed his favorite meal of pizza with chocolate cake for dessert.

By 9 PM, Ralph wanted to go to bed, but he didn't want to admit he was exhausted. By then, he had collected another 23 hugs, 28 Hershey Kisses, and 22 high-fives.

So even though it was 9 PM, Ralph kept playing the game; but believe it or not, he even started leaving hints about where he was hiding. You know what I mean—he would pretend to hide behind the sofa but leave one little front paw showing. Or he would leave his striped tail sticking out of the closet door. He was actually glad when someone found him and he could collect his hug, his high-five, or his Hershey Kiss.

At midnight, Ralph said with a sigh, "OK, I'm tired of playing the game."

The people of Happy Hollow Boarding School said, "Are you sure? We will play all night if you want us too. We won't give up and stop the game until you are sure you are ready."

"I'm sure," said Ralph as he started up the stairs to bed, but he was too tired to walk. His little feet were so heavy and he was falling asleep. Someone kindly picked him up in their arms and carried him up to his room.

As Ralph laid his little striped head down on his pillow he said, "OK, I'm done with running away. I know you'll find me and bring me back, wherever I go. But please tell me when I'm going to get to go back home."

"Well," said the Happy Hollow Boarding School staff person, "when it's the right time, and your parents are ready, you'll go home. Until then, perhaps we can be your home away from home—the next best thing to living at home."

With that, Ralph fell sound asleep. He was actually glad that the game was over. In the weeks ahead, he played "hide and go seek" once or twice, but he only used his favorite hiding places, where he was easily found. He liked knowing that if he could not be living at his home, living at Happy Hollow Boarding School was the next best thing.

THE BOTTOM LINE: Give up the game!

Treatment Interventions

Attachment Hide and Seek

This game reenacts the toddler attachment process, by allowing the child to run off and ensuring a safe return. Many traumatized children go through the attachment process at later ages than would be developmentally expected, so it is important for caregivers to follow the child's lead and be a loving, secure base to which the child may return. The game is useful with children that frequently run off or display ambivalence toward adults.

1. Therapist and child come up with agreed-upon places the child will use as running/hiding places (three for practicing at the therapy location and three at home).
2. Therapist gives child three poker chips labeled with *Hide #1, Hide #2,* and *Hide #3* written on them.
3. Therapist tells the child, "During our practice session today, when you are ready to hide, give me one of these tokens. I'll hold it in my hand and count to 25. Then I will come find you."
4. Play the game—when therapist finds the child, the child can choose a high-five, a hug, or an M&M chocolate (candy).
5. Therapist instructs child that during the week, when he/she feels like running, he must give a token to a parent before running to hide. Parents will find the child as quickly as possible.
6. When parent finds the child, child can choose a high-five, a hug, or an M&M chocolate (candy) to receive from the adult.
7. The child agrees to run away no more than three times a week. Parents may set limits on times for child to run, such as after school, after dinner, or before bedtime.
8. If child runs without leaving the token clue, he or she pays a consequence—upon returning to the house, the child must forfeit a run token.

Very Special Delivery

In many abusive/neglectful families, the parents put their needs before those of their children. This intervention reenacts the early attachment process in parent-child sessions and puts the child first. It helps "connect" children with attachment figures, particularly children who have learned to withdraw or isolate for self-protection. The parent figure may be a parent, foster parent, or child-care staff person.

1. Give parent and child some markers and paper, or a small dry erase board. The therapist serves as the postal delivery person.

2. Therapist (or child) attaches a long phone cord or yarn to the wrist of the child and the other end to the parent. Stretchy key chains are a great way to attach the cord to the wrists.
3. Ask the child to "leave" the parent and go just far enough to be out of sight but able to feel a tug on the wrist connection. The child may peek out or check on the parent; but the parent and child stay apart, out of sight from one another.
4. Therapist asks the child to write a message to the parent (or color a picture), then to tug on the rope and shout, "Special delivery!" Parent tugs back to show that he or she is ready for the delivery.
5. The therapist carries the mail to the parent, who carefully reads the child's message.
6. The parent responds to the mail with a positive note or picture to send back to the child.
7. The parent tugs on the cord, shouts, "Very special delivery." The child tugs back to show that he or she is ready for the delivery.
8. The therapist carries the mail to the child.
9. The process continues, and each time mail goes back and forth, another *very* is added to the list.
10. After several rounds of communication, ask the parent to go "find" the child and bring him/her closer.
11. Ask the parent and child to talk about which messages they liked best.
12. To end, let the child tell the parent what message he or she would most like to receive: "I wish you would say . . ." Let the parent send that as the final message.

The Power of Attraction

1. Using heavy cardboard, cut out a Ralph character and two adult characters. Decorate.
2. Glue strong magnets on the backs.
3. Measure how far apart the children and adults need to be to no longer feel a magnetic pull.
4. Measure how close they need to be to pull together.
5. Ask child what affects the strength of the pull between Ralph and the other characters.
6. Ask the child to "hide" the Ralph figure, far outside the magnetic pull.
7. Have the parent and adult "find" the Ralph figure and get close enough to pull him to them. Offer the child a hug, high-five, or Hershey Kiss.

8. Tell the child to hide the Ralph figure again, close to the pull of the magnet.
9. Ask the adult to tell Ralph that he or she must stay close enough to still feel the magnetic pull.
10. Ask how this feels different than letting Ralph hide far away.

Parent Promises

In parent group or parent individual therapy:

1. Ask parents to read the promises below and circle the ones they have made to their children.
2. Ask them to put an *x* by the promises that they believe they kept.
3. Ask them to put a star by the ones they did not keep.
4. Talk about any distortions, based on what is known about the parent's behavior.
5. Ask the parents to indicate promises they would like to make to their children and how their behavior would look if they kept those promises.

In child's group, have the children do the same: circle promises their parents have made; put an *x* by promises their parents kept; and put a star by promises their parents did not keep.

Initiate discussion about how children feel when adults do and don't carry out their promises. The children may then be asked to list promises that they believe are most important for adults to make and keep.

Promises
I love you just the way you are.
I will help you if you want my help.
I want you to tell me the truth about how I behave.
I want you to tell me when I disappoint, scare, or hurt you
I will not stop loving you—there is nothing you can do to lose my love.
What happened in our family was not your fault.
I'm sorry I did things that hurt or scared you.
I won't compete with you.
I'll set a good example by the things I do and say.
I won't let you hurt yourself or anyone else.
I won't let anyone hurt you.
I will not let you be the adult even if you demand, act bossy, or expect me to give in.
I will take care of our home and prepare meals.
I won't let you "take care of" me—I'll take care of you.

If I'm in a bad mood, I won't take it out on you!
I'll forgive you when you make a mistake.
I respect your feelings and your right to privacy.
I will enforce the rules and try to be consistent.
I will spend time with you and our family.
I'll compliment you and praise you every day!

Take-It-Home Discussion Questions

Therapist may assign one or more of the following questions for the child to answer and discuss with parent, foster parent, or staff or prior to the next session.

Do I ever feel I can't do anything right?
Do my parents act like they expect me to be perfect?
Why did Ralph run away? Did that solve his problem?
How do I act when I feel rejected?
When did I feel let down by someone else?
What would I do if I were Ralph?
Did my parents do things that made me feel unwanted?
Who do I turn to for hugs and high-fives?

BUILDING POSITIVE ATTACHMENT

Parents raised under less-than-ideal circumstances may have unusual views of how to raise children. Children require consistent adult nurture and protection to develop secure attachment. This laughable story (see chapter 2, page 42) illustrates how a mother receives help in learning to protect and nurture her children. The metaphor is easily translated into "real" parent-child relationship issues.

Treatment Intervention

Stick with It!

1. Help children create a large Velma doll out of cardboard. Ask them to draw some of their parent's features on the doll. Help the children glue pieces of soft Velcro on the doll.
2. On a piece of paper, ask the children to list things a parent does or says that make it hard for children to trust him or her (things that make kids feel angry, sad, scared, or confused). For younger children, describe it as types of touch, tone of voice, things parents say, and things parents do that can make the child feel bad.

3. On another piece of paper, ask the children to list things a parent does that make a child feel loved, happy, secure, and safe. Ask them to talk about why it is a good thing for babies to be close to their mothers and not get too far away.
4. Buy Ping-Pong balls to be the babies. Using permanent marker, draw on wings, eyes, beaks, and feathers. Glue Velcro strips on them.
5. Allow the children to throw the babies at the mother, suggesting they do it gently enough for the balls to stick. Point out that it is a good thing for babies to be close to their mother, in order to be safe and get fed.
6. Therapist pretends to be the parent doll and says or does something on one of the lists. If it is a positive attachment behavior, the child may throw a baby Ping-Pong ball to stick to the mother. If it is not a positive behavior, the child should hold the Ping-Pong ball.
7. Therapist praises children for knowing the difference and gives feedback as needed.
8. In parent group, after reading the story, ask parents to share anything that came up for them during the story. Next, ask them to list what they do to show love for their children and keep them close. Discuss. Following that discussion, ask parents to talk about things they do when they feel frustrated or overwhelmed by their children—things that may push them away or ways they expect them to take care of themselves. Ask the parents to come up with what else they might do under those circumstances to deal with their own frustration and not take it out on their children.

8

Changing Depressed Mood

Depression and mood disorders are common responses to childhood abuse and neglect. Children tend to blame themselves for negative life events (such as being placed in foster care or the family breaking up), and their distorted beliefs make it difficult for them to develop a positive sense of self, others, and the world. Children rarely understand that thoughts, feelings, and life events are connected. Therapy provides an opportunity for children to challenge distorted beliefs and develop self-efficacy.

Depressed children and teens may develop learned helplessness, an external locus of control, and pessimism about life in general. Depressed children display a variety of symptoms. Some are grouchy and irritable. Others are sad and withdrawn. Many depressed children voice negative thoughts and think that others don't like them. They may feel picked on and think they have no friends.

Compared with non-depressed peers, depressed children devalue themselves in valued life areas such as school ability (smartness), physical prowess (strength), physical appearance, and being popular (liked by others). They have low self-efficacy and low self-confidence.

It is important to treat childhood depression, since many depressed children grow up to be depressed adults. Therapists can help depressed children challenge negative views of self and others; focus on positive events and success; and seek opportunities for social development using cognitive behavioral and play therapies. Through effective treatment, children can build positive self-esteem, challenge irrational beliefs, and learn to better control their emotions and behaviors.

MOOD MANAGEMENT

Barry the Basset Hound in *The Black Cloud*, the story that follows, has a black cloud that follows him around when he becomes depressed. Like others who are depressed, Barry at first perceives his feelings as coming out of nowhere; with the help of a friend, he realizes he can monitor, control, and change his own thoughts and feelings.

The story provides an introduction to CBT, and the exercises will allow a depressed child to practice the concepts in the story. Barry provides a good model for the life events-thoughts-feelings process. Depressed children will identify with him as they develop new coping strategies.

THE BLACK CLOUD

It was finally Saturday, and Barry the Basset Hound was alone in his room. In case you didn't know, a basset hound is a type of dog with short legs and very droopy ears and eyes. Barry wanted everyone to leave him alone, because it had been a very bad week.

"What a terrible week this has been! I'm no good," moaned Barry. "I can't do anything right."

On Monday, Barry had an "accident" on the kitchen floor (that means he could not wait to go to the bathroom and did it in the kitchen instead of outside) and his mother growled at him.

On Tuesday, Barry barked in the middle of the night and woke up his parents. They were not very happy and made him sleep in the basement. He usually got to sleep in their bedroom.

On Wednesday, Barry ate something he shouldn't (a dead mouse the cat brought home) and threw up all over the rug.

On Thursday, the dogs at school laughed at him (for about the hundredth time) for having long ears. Sometimes he was clumsy and tripped on his ears when he walked—it was so embarrassing!

On Friday, Barry's dad lost his job as a school guard dog. He had worked there ten years sniffing out drugs from the school lockers. The school budget got cut (that means they ran out of money), so the school could no longer pay him.

Now it was Saturday, and Barry's dad was grouchy, his mom was howling a lot (basset hounds howl with a very sad-sounding moan), and Barry doubted that things were going to get better any time soon. He spent the whole day in his room, with his tail tucked between his legs.

The next day, Sunday, arrived cloudy and raining, and it turned out to be another bad day. On Sunday afternoon, Barry chewed the leg of his mother's favorite chair leg, without even thinking.

"Naughty dog!" howled his mother.

When Monday came, he said to his mother, "I don't want to go to school." His mother said, "You're not throwing up and you don't have a fever, so you have to go to school."

"You are the meanest mom in the whole world," cried Barry.

"Maybe I am, but you are going to school," replied his mother.

When he got home from school, his mother saw the frown on Barry's face and asked, "How was your day?"

"It was bad," he said. "I'm stupid, ugly, and no one likes me!"

Barry's mother replied, "You are fine just the way you are. I'm sure tomorrow will be better."

"Nobody knows how I feel—not even you!" Barry barked at his mother as he ran to his room. Barry sulked all the way there, dragging his long ears on the floor.

Then it was Tuesday again. On Tuesday, Barry woke up with an upset stomach and a howling headache. He threw up right after eating his dog chow breakfast.

"My life sucks," Barry moaned as he went back to bed after throwing up. Barry knew that "sucks" was a bad word, and that's exactly why he said it.

"Watch your language!" warned his mother. "Just because you're sick doesn't give you an excuse to talk like that!"

This time, Barry's mother let him stay home from school, because he was really sick and not just "faking it." For three days, Barry was sick and didn't go to school. He slept a lot and kept the shade pulled down in his dark room. Barry had three whole days to think about how bad his life was.

On Friday, Barry's mother woke him up for school and said, "Come eat your breakfast. You are well enough to go back to school."

Barry felt very grouchy that morning. He whined, "Can't I please stay home from school just one more day?"

"No, Barry," replied his mother. "You have already missed a lot of school." His mother licked his fur lovingly and fed him a good breakfast of special dog chow with meat chunks. She gave him a small nip on the back of his neck to hurry him out the door, and Barry shivered in the cool air.

"My life is full of gloom and doom," Barry said with a sigh as he walked to school. "I am a dog with a lot of bad luck, and nothing I do is going to make it any better."

As Barry said that, a small gray cloud appeared over his head. It was light gray, just like the clouds that come out on a morning when it might rain later that day.

Then Barry said, "*No one* likes me, and *nothing* I do is going to make that any better." As Barry said *that*, the small cloud grew darker. It was now a very dark gray cloud, just like the clouds that appear right before a thunderstorm.

Finally Barry said, his eyes drooping, "I wish I had *never been born.* My parents would be better off without me." With these words, the cloud turned dark black, just like the clouds that shut out the sunshine right before a horrible tornado.

It was a sunny day outside, but the cloud over Barry's head blocked out the sunlight like an eclipse. In case you do not know it, an eclipse is when the moon comes directly between the earth and the sun—when that happens you can't see the sun even though it is still there.

With the black cloud over his head, all Barry could see was darkness. Others could see the sun, but Barry's black cloud blocked the sun completely.

Over the next few weeks, the black cloud went everywhere with Barry. When Barry got home from school each day, his mother barked, "Barry, come play fetch with me!"

Barry howled back, "I'm tired, Mom. I'm going to take a quick dognap." He spent most of his time alone in his room. He was very tired (even when he got lots of sleep), and he wanted to sleep a lot.

When Barry's brother stuck his long nose in Barry's food dish, Barry didn't bark at him like he usually did, to chase him away. Barry had pretty much lost his appetite.

Barry said, "Oh go ahead. I don't care if you eat my food. I'm not very hungry." His brother cocked his head in surprise and gobbled up all the food in Barry's food dish.

You might wonder why Barry didn't tell anyone how bad he felt. Well, mainly he didn't want to bother anyone with his problems. "My parents have problems of their own," he thought. "What could they do anyway?" he wondered. "My life is pretty hopeless!" Barry believed that no matter what he did, his life wasn't going to get any better. To Barry, it seemed like forever since he had seen the sunshine.

Then one Saturday, his friend Fred the Beagle came over to visit. Fred barked to Barry, "Excuse me for being nosy, but why don't you get rid of that black cloud?"

Barry gave a mournful howl. "I don't have any control over the black cloud."

Fred disagreed, "I think you're wrong. I notice that when you smile and say something nice or positive, the cloud gets lighter. When you say something grouchy or negative, the cloud gets darker. Maybe if you change what you think and say, the cloud will go away."

Barry did not believe his friend, but he decided to give it a try.

First Barry said something very hopeless: "I wish I had never been born!" The cloud turned black.

Then he complained about the weather: "I hate rainy days." The cloud turned a lighter gray.

Finally he said something very positive: "I'm glad Fred is such a nice friend!" The cloud turned fluffy and white. His friend was right!

"I guess I do have control over the cloud," thought Barry. He *was* tired of having it over his head all the time. He couldn't change what happened in his life, but maybe he could change how he reacted. While his friend Fred watched, Barry practiced saying things in a more positive way.

He changed, "No one likes me" to "Some kids don't like me, and others do." Instead of saying, "Things will never get better," he said, "I will do what I can to make things better." Each time Barry changed his words, the cloud over his head got lighter. It was amazing!

His friend Fred added, "You might want to get out in the sun more, Barry. Fresh air and exercise will give you more energy. Everyone knows that staying inside and acting lazy makes you really tired." Then Fred barked, "Barry, I have to go home now to eat my dog chow and practice chasing my tail. See you tomorrow at school."

Barry started doing what his friend Fred had suggested. He walked to and from school, kept his thoughts more positive, and played outside every day after school. He discovered that the fresh air and exercise helped his mood, and within two weeks, the black cloud had nearly disappeared.

One day soon after, Barry got home from school and barked at his mother. "Come on, Mom," he said. "Let's go play fetch!" His mother yipped with pleasure and nipped at Barry's feet as they ran outside to play together.

When his brother tried to gobble up Barry's food that night, Barry growled at him and chased him back to his own food dish. "Oh good," thought his brother, "Barry's back to his old self again!"

You might want to know how this story ends. Well, Barry's father got a new job as a school crossing guard, his mother howled much less, and Barry had some good days and some bad days, just like everyone else. After all, there is really no such thing as "happily ever after." Sometimes his black cloud came back when he had a bad day (when he didn't notice what he was thinking and saying), but he no longer let it color his life in the way it had before.

THE BOTTOM LINE: Do something to lighten up!

Treatment Interventions

Lighten Your Cloud

Therapist gives each family member several copies of the Cloud Worksheet on page 114 and a black crayon or gray and black markers.

Individual Cloud Statements
1. Instructions: Take a cloud worksheet. Write something *really* negative you might think or say about yourself or your life when you are very sad, irritable, or depressed. Perhaps think of the most hopeless or depressed thing you have ever said to yourself. Now, color the cloud black. Write down how this makes you feel.
2. Now take another cloud worksheet. Change the first statement slightly to make it less negative (perhaps take out a word such as "always" or "never" or "no one"), write it in the second bubble, and color the cloud gray. Write down how this makes you feel.
3. Now on a third cloud worksheet, write a positive statement about yourself or your life in the third bubble that contradicts the negative statements. Add some hope or qualify the negative statements. Leave the third cloud white. Write down how the positive statements make you feel.
4. Do you see any connection between what you say to yourself and how you feel?
5. Describe a time when you changed your mood by something you thought or said.

Family Cloud Statements
1. Ask the family to think about good and bad things they could say about their family.
2. Ask them to use cloud worksheets—color one cloud black, color one gray, and leave one white.
3. Ask family members to make a list of very negative statements about the family (angry, depressed, disgusted, hopeless, etc.) under the black cloud.
4. Then ask family members to write statements under the gray cloud that are a little less negative about the family situation.
5. Lastly, ask family members to write positive, true, rational, hopeful statements about the family under the white cloud.
6. Discuss how thinking affects feelings in family members.

CLOUD WORKSHEET

Take-It-Home Discussion Questions

Therapist may assign one or more of the following questions for the child to answer and discuss with parent, foster parent, or staff or prior to the next session.

How am I like Barry?

What advice do I have for Barry?

When I think about myself, compared to other kids, do I think I am better, worse, or about the same, in my looks? How smart I am? How talented, physically strong, athletic am I? How good am I at making and keeping friends, at being popular?

When I had a very bad day, what was happening and how did I feel?

Pretend you are Barry and practice changing the color of your cloud.

When do I have a black cloud over my head? What brings sunshine into my life?

What do I need to do to get into the "sunshine" more?

In what ways do I judge that I am unacceptable?

What can I do to "lighten up"?

9

Empathy

Caring for Yourself and Others

The capacity for empathy, being able to put yourself in "someone else's shoes," grows out of secure parent-child attachment. In order to care for others, a child must first be the recipient of consistent, loving care. Social and cognitive competencies go hand in hand with healthy emotional development. Abuse and neglect may "stunt" cognitive, social, and emotional development. Therapy helps remediate these delays, enabling children to develop age-appropriate empathy.

One of the ideas behind empathy is that it is hard to pass it on to others if you did not get it yourself. This concept is a little like the Hebrew concept of the blessing. In the book *Gift of the Blessing* (Smalley & Trent 1993), the authors discuss the tradition of the Hebrew blessing.

According to Hebrew tradition, a blessing includes five ingredients: meaningful touch, spoken word, expressing high value, picturing a special future, and an active commitment. The main concept of the book is that once we have been blessed, we will respond to the blessing and be able to pass on the blessing to others. Smalley and Trent point out that it is easier to pass on the blessing to our children when we have first received the blessing (unconditional love) from our parents. The capacity for empathy (feeling what someone else feels by being able to take his or her perspective) develops as a result of caregiver unconditional love.

The "Love thy neighbor as thyself" statement from the Bible assumes that one will love self first, and then, as a result, develop the capacity to love others. Before children can understand and be sensitive to the feelings of others, they must be recipients of love and acceptance. Children develop positive self-esteem through consistent and loving attention. And if they do not receive consistent or loving attention as children, abused individuals may not know how to relate to or care for others when they grow up.

Meaningful touch is gentle, caring touch that builds trust. Spoken word indicates that we must tell others that we love them. Expressing high value means that we must convey our positive regard to those we love. Picturing a special future is the capacity to tell our children we believe in them and their talents, and we are confident in their future success. An active commitment means that we will be good role models, understanding that children will do what we do, not what we say. And we promise to be there for them even when they make mistakes.

Persons without the capacity for empathy often have serious pathology and are insensitive to the feelings of others. They disregard societal rules and may develop opportunistic attitudes or conduct-disordered behaviors. Children without empathy may be sneaky and prey on those that are vulnerable, such as animals or other young children.

Treatment interventions help children be sensitive to their own feelings and to the feelings of those around them. By offering parents "the blessing" and teaching them how to pass it on, we provide relationship skills that will be the building blocks for relationships in years to come.

HEARTBREAK

The Girl with the Plastic Heart is a story written for pre-teens or teens that are bitter about being hurt and start to take out their hurt on others. The metaphor of the plastic heart was a 17-year-old girl's explanation for her sarcastic, mean attitude toward staff and peers. With her permission, the author included it in a story about her. She pretended it was no big deal, but later she read it to her mother on the phone, the same mother that had abandoned her so cruelly. The story has enough humor in it to appeal to teens, and it leads nicely into exploration of deeper feelings.

The story encourages teens to reopen their hearts when they have been hurt, be willing to trust again, and allow themselves to love and be loved.

THE GIRL WITH THE PLASTIC HEART (dedicated to P)

A teenage girl and her friend were walking down the sidewalk on a bright sunny day. As they approached an older woman, the woman smiled and said, "Hi, how are you today?" and stepped aside to let the girls pass.

The girl smirked at her friend as if to say, "Just watch what I'm going to do!" She frowned at the woman and said in a rude voice, "What's it to you? Go away and mind your own business, old lady."

As if that wasn't enough, she deliberately bumped the startled woman hard enough to knock her off balance. The woman had to step off the sidewalk into the muddy grass to avoid falling.

The girl's friend helped the woman back onto the sidewalk as her friend walked briskly ahead. She explained, "Don't mind her. She knocks *everyone* off balance."

"And why is that?" asked the woman.

The friend replied, "It's because she has a plastic heart."

"A plastic heart?" the woman asked.

"Yes," replied the girl's friend. "Her real heart is on vacation."

"Why did her heart go on vacation?" the woman asked.

"Well," said the friend, "her real heart got broken over and over by those she loved—especially by her mother. It needed a rest and time to heal."

"When someone breaks your heart," said the woman, "you need to find love somewhere else, to help your heart heal."

The friend replied sadly, "A heart that gets broken many times takes longer and longer to heal. My friend's real heart was becoming scarred from all the hurt and sadness. So she replaced it with a plastic heart. A plastic heart has no feeling—that's why she says or does whatever she pleases."

"Was sending her heart on vacation her only choice?" asked the woman.

The friend replied, "The doctor wanted her to keep her real heart and take better care of it. Her friends suggested she avoid people that had broken her heart. But my friend is very stubborn. She thinks she knows what's best for her."

The woman's face grew concerned. "Hearts on vacation grow lazy, and it's hard to convince them to come home. Let's go talk to your friend."

The woman and the girl's friend ran to catch up with the girl with the plastic heart.

"What do *you* want?" the girl asked her friend. "And why is that ugly old woman with you?"

The friend replied, "I told her about your plastic heart."

"My plastic heart is none of her business," said the girl.

"That may be true," interrupted the woman. "But I have to tell you something."

The girl rolled her eyes and said, "OK, old woman, tell me—I'm sure it will be something stupid."

The woman spoke quickly. "Your heart belongs with you—not at a vacation resort. Hearts on vacation become lazy and selfish. Your real heart is probably complaining to everyone that you are a heartless person for sending it away and forgetting about it."

The girl frowned and looked annoyed. "I'm going to give my heart a piece of my mind!" she exclaimed. "Let's go!"

They all traveled to the tropical island resort where the real heart was staying. The woman had been right. The heart was sitting by the side of a pool, all flabby and lazy, wearing glittery sunglasses and sipping a fruity drink.

"Where have you been and what do you want?" the real heart asked the girl in an annoyed voice.

The girl decided it was time to end the heart's vacation. "Your vacation is over—it's time to go home and get back to work."

"You don't need *me*," said the heart. "You have that cheap plastic model."

"The plastic heart is brittle and cracked," said the girl.

"Well, I don't know if I *want* to come back," said the heart. "I could have helped you make friends or find real love. But nooooo, you had to replace me!" Then the heart took a really cheap shot. "You're no better than the people that broke *your* heart. You sent me away and forgot about me!"

"I'm not like the people that broke my heart!" said the girl. "I'm loyal and dependable, and I keep my promises. I care about others, even though I may not always show it."

She added, "I sent you away on vacation so that you could heal, and you have healed just fine. So pack your things. You're coming home with me." The heart realized it did not have a choice and went to pack.

While the real heart was packing, the woman came over and handed the girl a soft scarf. "Here," said the woman. "It's a heart-warmer, to protect your real heart from being broken. I want you to have it."

The real heart returned with her suitcase, ready to go home with the girl. The girl wrapped her real heart gently in the heart warmer and quickly replaced the plastic heart.

"There," she said. "That's better."

Inside the girl, the real heart whispered something to her that no one else could hear.

"I almost forgot," the girl said as she spoke to the woman. "Thanks for the heart-warmer. I'm sorry I was so hard-hearted before!"

"That's OK," said the woman. "I understand."

The woman said good-bye to the girl and her friend. She saw a visible difference in the girl now that her real heart was back in place. She knew that the heart-warmer would protect the girl from hurt.

Later, the girl wondered what had happened to the brittle plastic heart with all the cracks in it. The girl would never know it, but the woman had spoken the truth when she said, "I understand."

Believe it or not, the girl's plastic heart was sitting on a shelf in the old woman's house. It sat right next to a second cracked plastic heart and a photo of the woman's real heart lazing away at a tropical resort.

THE BOTTOM LINE: Don't set your heart aside!

Treatment Interventions

In these exercises, parents are encouraged to show empathy for their children's feelings about having been hurt; and children gain closure over past hurts.

Heart to Heart

1. Make a list of things you imagine the girl's mother did to break her heart.
2. Draw a broken heart, and write inside it the things that broke the girl's heart.
3. Write a letter from the girl to her mother, telling her what she did to break her heart.
4. Have the girl add to her letter what she wishes her mother would do to help "heal" the hurt.

Walking in Each Other's Shoes (May Be Done with Family or Group)

This exercise encourages family members to show empathy toward one another.

1. Therapist asks each person to trace his or her shoes while standing on a piece of mural or poster paper. Ask members to decorate their drawn shoes to match the actual shoes they are wearing that day.
2. Therapist asks each person to write his or her name on the paper by the shoes.
3. Therapist asks each person to write down, by the shoes, one thing he or she is burdened by/worrying about or a bad memory that makes him/her feel bad.
4. Therapist asks family members to share what they have written.
5. Instructions: "Go ahead and take one step to the right and stand under the next person's shoes. Imagine you are now walking in that person's shoes. Try to picture how that person feels about the thing they wrote on the paper. Please write down a short message of support or encouragement for that person and sign your name. Try to make the support specific to the issue that person wrote down."
6. After continuing to step to the right, one set of footsteps at a time, and writing comments, have a family discussion about how it feels to see things from someone else's point of view and how it feels to see the support of family members.
7. Process how family members generally do or do not support one another in daily life.

Make It Better

Everyone remembers the toddler coming to the parent saying, "I fell down." A common parent response is, "Let me kiss it and make it better," which is followed by loving attention to the "boo-boo." Children often keep their hurts to themselves when parents are inaccessible or inattentive. It is important that children be able to come to their parents for comfort and that their parents respond with nurturing behaviors.

1. Child does a body tracing and draws a large valentine heart on the body where the heart would be.
2. Therapist then asks child to select a different color marker for each person who hurt his or her feelings or broke his or her heart.
3. Child uses the chosen color and writes each name or initials under the heart.
4. Therapist asks child to talk about what people did or said that hurt the child's feelings and/or broke the child's heart.
5. Therapist explains that family members can help one another feel better, and replace hurts with love.
6. Therapist gives out small Band-Aids and heart-shaped stickers to the child, who tells the parent what kind of response he or she needs/wants.
7. Ask the parent to respond to the child's hurt verbally and to put a Band-Aid and sticker on the child's heart.

The Blessing

This intervention is adapted from *The Blessing* (Smalley & Trent 1993). Therapist asks family members to answer and discuss their answers to the following questions.

Meaningful Touch
1. Child—Give an example of a time your parent(s) used gentle, kind touch. How did it make you feel?
2. Parent—Give an example of a time you used gentle, kind touch with your child. How did your child respond?

Spoken Word
1. Child—Give an example of a time your parent(s) said, "I love you." How did it make you feel?
2. Parent—Give an example of a time you told your child, "I love you." How did your child respond?

Expressing High Value
1. Child—Give an example of a time your parent(s) used praise toward you. How did it make you feel?
2. Parent—Give an example of a time you used praise toward your child. How did your child respond?

Picturing a Special Future
1. Child—Give an example of a time your parent(s) predicted that you would be successful or have a special future. How did that make you feel?
2. Parent—Give an example of a time you predicted to your child that he or she would be successful or have a special future. How did your child respond?

An Active Commitment
1. Child—Give an example of a time your parent(s) were "there for you" during a really tough time. How did that make you feel?
2. Parent—Give an example of a time you were there for your child during a really tough time. How did your child respond?

The Family Blessing   Write a family blessing on a piece of paper. Decorate it with markers and glitter glue. Be sure it has all the elements of a blessing. Each person should contribute something to the family blessing.

Take-It-Home Discussion Questions

Therapist may assign one or more of the following questions for the child to answer and discuss with parent, foster parent, or staff or prior to the next session.

How are the plastic heart and the real heart different?
Did I ever act mad when my feelings were hurt?
What does the girl need to do to heal her broken heart?
Why does the woman understand how the girl feels?
Am I more like the girl with the plastic heart, her friend, or the woman?
How do I react when someone I love hurts me?
Have I ever had my heart broken by someone I loved?
Who or what is my heart-warmer?

10

Responsibility and Accountability

The following statements were taken from session notes:

"If he was hurting you, you should have spoken up."

"It's your fault you never said anything."

"You shouldn't have turned on the stove while I was asleep"

"You shouldn't have left the house when I wasn't home."

"I know I shouldn't have let him come back but he had no place to go—he's the father of my kids."

"My meth use only got BAD after my mother died."

"I don't know how he got his hands on the lighter—he must have gone through my purse."

"I would be a good parent if they would just behave."

"I was right next door—they could come get me if they needed me" (mother of four young children).

"They should know better than to talk back when he's (I'm) in a bad mood."

According to the transtheoretical model of change (Prochaska & Velicer 1997), many court-referred individuals are in the pre-contemplation stage when they begin treatment. It is easy to see from the statements above that some parents have difficulty accepting responsibility for their choices and actions.

Abusive and neglectful parents often blame and excuse their own inappropriate behavior. They focus on the reasons they did or didn't do things, at times subtly blaming the children or others for consequences of their own choices. Therapy helps such parents verbalize responsibility for their decisions and behavior; apologize to their children for past choices; and demonstrate in their current behavior a genuine commitment to change.

Children often believe they were removed from the home for misbehaving or for being "bad" and think they *deserved* what happened to them. They regret *telling* and feel responsible for *breaking up the family*. Siblings who were abused together or forced to witness/participate in sexual activities experience shame, rage, helplessness, and survivor guilt. Siblings may blame one another (instead of perpetrators) for past abuse and find it hard to move toward recovery.

The entire family must recognize that parents are the ones accountable for child behavior management, safety, and nurturance. Children need to understand that parents must be *stable enough to manage the variations in behavior and emotion shown by their children.* When parents blame their children, or drinking, or mental health, or fatigue for parental loss of control, therapists remind them that many families in the community deal effectively with these issues without hurting their children. Children need to be told clearly that it was not their fault they experienced, participated in, or witnessed abuse. Cognitive restructuring helps children address issues of loyalty, shame, guilt, betrayal, and helplessness.

Therapists may wish to suggest that parents consider what they *can* change rather than obsessing about things that are outside their control. It is not helpful for families to bitterly rehash perceived injustices. Therapists need not placate parents who are experiencing genuine remorse at losing the trust of their children. Part of the treatment process is helping parents forgive themselves.

Treatment will not be effective unless the adults in the family verbalize responsibility for their decisions and behavior; apologize to their children for past behavior; and demonstrate (in their actions) a commitment to change.

Some families target one or another child as the "problem child" and blame the family or marital problems on that child's behavior. Interestingly though, the targeted child may change from one "crisis" to the next. We have used the metaphor of the carnival game where the little gopher heads pop up and down while you try to bop them quickly with a padded club to obtain points. Therapists can point out that children's problems are like the gophers. Each child's issues will "pop up" at one point or another, and parents need to keep "bopping" the problems (not the children!) as they arise, one at a time, figuratively speaking. It's not fair to target one family member as "the problem"; in fact, the gopher heads are connected (like a family system) and they will continue taking turns until the "game" is over!

The stories and activities in this chapter help parents consider how their behavior has affected their children; and they help the children think about how they have been affected by their parents' choices and behaviors, both omissions and commissions.

EXTERNALIZING BLAME

Use the story *Bear of a Different Color*, found on p. 11 of chapter 1.

Treatment Interventions

Get Ready to Get Mad!

Return to the bear story and the child's body tracing.

1. Ask the child who Bear might be mad at for falling in the hole.
2. Discuss with the child what went wrong or happened in the story that led to Bear's fall.
3. Ask the child what went wrong in his or her family that led to the abuse or neglect.
4. Ask the child if he or she is "mad" at anyone for what happened in his/her family.
5. As the child talks about each "black goop" area on the body tracing, help the child disclose details about prior abuse, including how he/she was hurt and who hurt him/her.
6. Each perpetrator's name is put on the "Mad List" (see below).

The Mad List

Use this technique to create a "Mad List" (or a "Sad, Hurt, or Scared List").

1. At any point where the child shares the name of a perpetrator, therapist helps the child begin constructing a "Mad List" (see page 128). Most children will voice anger at their perpetrators. Some will voice sadness, hurt, or fear, and those feelings may be added to the title of the list.
2. As the child shares names of perpetrators, therapist can ask about the child's perceptions. It is important to understand how the child viewed the person before the abuse, during the abuse, and after the abuse. It is also important to ascertain how the child feels now in terms of safety, future risk, level of guilt, etc.
3. The child is reminded that the "Mad List" is for all the names of the persons that hurt him or her, physically, emotionally, or sexually, due to abuse or neglect. Therapist can educate child that hurt can be to your feelings, your body, or your brain (makes you worry or makes it hard for you to sleep). The "Mad List" becomes a running list to use with the next intervention, "Your Day in Court."

YOUR MAD LIST

Name: _____ Date:_____

You might have "mad" (or "sad" or "scared") feelings about people in the past that abused or neglected you. It's OK to feel really mad about being abused or neglected. Your Mad List is the people in your past that were mean to you and hurt you through abuse or neglect. It is OK to put the MAD where it belongs—on this list! Don't put down names of people that you get mad at for everyday reasons—you know, like a friend who hurt your feelings or made you feel left out, or someone who told you "no" or asked you to do something you didn't want to do. Those names don't belong on the "mad list." Just write down the names of people that abused or neglected you in the past.

_____
_____
_____
_____
_____
_____
_____
_____
_____
_____
_____
_____
_____
_____
_____
_____
_____
_____
_____

Your Day in Court

Most children become familiar with the court system as they go through the investigation process. They may have a CASA (court appointed special advocate), and each child is represented by an attorney. Many children eventually meet the family court judge. Children feel vulnerable, victimized, and helpless following abuse. "Your Day in Court" is about experiential participatory justice. This intervention allows a child to play judge and assign one or more punishments to the perpetrator. In doing so, children re-establish feelings of safety and control—the roles are reversed! The child experiences righteous indignation—justice will be done, at least here in the therapy room!

In this activity, the child selects the name of a perpetrator off the "Mad List." He or she completes a "crime list" by checking off the crimes that the person has committed (see Your Day in Court handout on page 130). Next, the child becomes the judge in a court of law. He or she "sentences" the perpetrator to fantasy-based punishments—most are ludicrous choices that will delight the child. Children with whom we have worked particularly enjoy the "poop-related" ones. Therapists should not confuse "play aggression" with actual "danger to others." Many children will assign very violent punishments, but their anger will dissipate as justice is carried out.

By taking the case to court, convicting the abuser of a crime, with the child as judge, the child is able to decrease affective arousal, increase self-efficacy, and reduce self-blame for what happened. Playing judge gives the child the clear message that the perpetrator is accountable for his or her behavior. The sentencing phase allows a child to feel creatively "in charge" as he/she plays out fantasy-based legal action.

A nine-year-old boy used his "Mad List" to put blame where it belonged. He took great delight in sentencing the adults and picking "punishments" for his perpetrators. He enacted various punishments in play therapy until he believed that they had gotten "what they deserved." As he (and his brother) blasted perpetrators into space, wrapped them in duct tape, and buried them in the sand tray over a period of two months, his anxiety and rage decreased dramatically. Interestingly, no one, including the CPS investigators, had been aware of this boy's sexual abuse until he completed the court and sentencing phase of the activity.

Therapists may find that use of this list continues throughout treatment, as new names will emerge and the story will unfold gradually. It is a powerful pair of interventions and allows for quite a bit of therapist and child creativity. Therapists should not be put off by the intensity of children's rage or sentencing that involves violence or the death penalty. Each child will deal with feelings of victimization in ways that best allow the rage to dissipate; and having the child serve as judge means that it is not the child who formally carries out the sentence.

YOUR DAY IN COURT

Your Name: _____

Mad List Person's Name: _____

In court, they charge the person with crimes (what the person did). What crimes do you charge this person with? Check all the things that this person did to you or made you do.

Did This to Me
- ☐ Left me all alone
- ☐ Hit, punched, slapped, or kicked me
- ☐ Touched my private part
- ☐ Burned or cut me
- ☐ Touched my butt
- ☐ Put their private part in my mouth, vagina, or butt
- ☐ Threatened, cursed, or screamed at me
- ☐ Took "dirty" pictures of me
- ☐ Got in bed, bath, or shower with me
- ☐ Put my face in poop
- ☐ Lied to me
- ☐ Gave me money for doing something they wanted me to do
- ☐ Kissed me
- ☐ Shoved me around
- ☐ Other: _____

Made Me Do This
- ☐ Touch their private part
- ☐ Steal
- ☐ Kiss them
- ☐ Touch someone else's private part
- ☐ Lie about something
- ☐ Keep secrets about what happened
- ☐ Watch or listen while they hurt someone
- ☐ Look at "dirty" pictures or movies
- ☐ Take my clothes off
- ☐ Take a bath or shower with them
- ☐ Put my private part in someone else
- ☐ Hurt someone while they watched
- ☐ Sleep with them or lay on top of them
- ☐ Use drugs or alcohol
- ☐ Deliver drugs to someone
- ☐ Have sex with someone else
- ☐ Other: _____

When the person is convicted (court decides that the person is guilty), the judge gives a consequence (the sentence). They have to pay for what they did. As the trial judge, what punishment (sentence) will you give this person? You can pick more than one and write your own.

- ☐ Life in prison
- ☐ Banish to distant planet
- ☐ Paralyze with poison darts
- ☐ "Freeze" them with magic
- ☐ Death penalty
- ☐ Lock them in a dungeon in chains
- ☐ Pour honey or caramel on them and cover them with biting ants
- ☐ Make them eat poop
- ☐ Fill their room w/mosquitoes
- ☐ Roll them in poop and feathers
- ☐ Make posters that say *Child Molester* with their picture on them
- ☐ Put their head underwater
- ☐ Make them swim in sewage
- ☐ Throw rotten eggs at them
- ☐ Shrink them and keep them in a hamster cage
- ☐ Other: _____

- ☐ Have their private parts removed
- ☐ Send away to live on deserted island
- ☐ Watch movie of me being happy (100 times)
- ☐ Read a book about my success (100 times)
- ☐ Take away their voice
- ☐ Use magic to make them disappear forever
- ☐ Wrap them in duct tape
- ☐ Make them go on TV and admit what they did
- ☐ Make them live in a room full of poop
- ☐ Make them live with a skunk
- ☐ Blast them into space
- ☐ Make them wear a dog collar and leash
- ☐ Write and sign a confession and apology
- ☐ Put them on Internet sex offender list
- ☐ Other: _____

Thank you for making this a safer place!

TAKING RESPONSIBILITY

Family members may blame "the system" or one another for what happened in the family. This amusing story focuses on not blaming others for your own problems. It also encourages honesty and openness in relationships.

Children need opportunities, often over and over, to see that they are not responsible for abuse or neglect. They benefit from having their caregivers take full responsibility for their choices.

The next story, *No More Blame Game*, presents Gilda Goose, a young-adult goose that holds grudges and blames others for her problems. She makes hasty decisions and is set in her ways, like many abusive or neglectful parents.

Gilda Goose, stubborn and independent, has trouble admitting her own shortcomings until she comes up against someone who knew her many years ago. Family members will chuckle at Gilda's antics and easily move into a discussion of owning and being responsible for their own choices.

NO MORE BLAME GAME

You might be tempted to stare at Gilda Goose if you saw her riding home from work on her large black motorcycle. However, I would recommend that you NOT stare.

The other day, Gilda caught Dahlia Duck staring at her. "HOOONNKK! WHAT DO YOU THINK YOU'RE LOOKING AT? MIND YOUR OWN BUSINESS!"

Poor Dahlia Duck was so startled! "Quaaaack," she cried as she flew up in the air about three feet.

I can understand why Dahlia stared at Gilda. It was not because Gilda was riding a motorcycle. Gilda had always ridden a motorcycle. It was just hard to ignore the big white cast on Gilda's foot, the huge bandage on her feathered head, and the elastic wrap around her wing. All that and dark goggles, too!

Gilda's motorcycle goggles were completely black, because she had never peeled the black film off the lenses. It was a protective covering and was labeled, "Remove at time of first use." Gilda didn't remove it, though, because she hated someone else telling her what to do.

As you might guess, it is hard to drive a motorcycle at night when you can't see through your goggles—that's probably why Gilda had hit a bump in the road, flown into a pine tree, and ended up in the emergency room. What a stubborn goose!

Gilda had another unusual habit. She never used a map when she traveled, even though she was a lifetime member of AAA, better known as "Triple A." AAA is an auto club that sends you all the free maps you want, but Gilda didn't want any. Instead of using a map, when Gilda came to a crossing in the road, she would honk, "Eenie, meenie, miney, moe." Wherever her wing pointed when she got to "moe"—that is where she turned. Each time Gilda got lost—and, as you may well imagine, she often got lost—she complained, "Those road crews should put up better signs!" *Then* Gilda called AAA on her cell phone to get directions.

Gilda also had the bad habit of holding grudges. She was still mad at Mrs. Pelican, her third-grade teacher. The teacher had sent her for tutoring, because Gilda could not read. Gilda hated tutoring and stopped after two weeks. Gilda never did her homework and still could not read or write by fourth grade, so she quit school. After Gilda quit school, she went to work, and she had worked ever since. Now, ten years later, Gilda still complained, honking loudly, "That awful teacher Mrs. Pelican. Because of her, I don't know how to read."

I hope you're getting the picture. Gilda was a stubborn goose that blamed others for her problems, and now she had a new problem. Her best friend Jenny was getting married in Florida, and she had invited Gilda to attend. She and Jenny had been fast-feathered friends ever since they met in the first grade. Gilda had never been to Florida, but she needed to get there in two days if she wanted to attend the wedding.

Gilda's doctor had told her she could take the trip if she promised not to get her cast wet. So Gilda put on her film-covered goggles and took off on her motorcycle without a map—soon she was totally lost. On top of all that, it was starting to rain, and her cast was going to get wet. "Oh my," she honked, "how am I ever going to find my way to Florida?"

Gilda pulled out her cell phone and was about to call AAA, when a large four-wheel drive pulled up and stopped behind her. Someone rolled down the driver's side window. "Gilda, is that you?" asked an older voice. "Are you lost?"

Gilda thought the person looked familiar and realized, "Oh no, it's old Julia Pelican, my first-grade teacher!"

"Yes, Mrs. Pelican," said Gilda Goose, "it's me, Gilda." Gilda did not want to admit that she was lost. "I'm not lost," she lied. "I'm just taking the scenic route."

In case you don't know it, the "scenic route" is the route you take when you are not in a hurry and want to do some sightseeing on your way. It is NOT the route you take when you are in a hurry and have only two days to get to a wedding.

"I'm driving down to Florida for Jenny's wedding," said Mrs. Pelican. "Would you like a ride? We could put your motorcycle in the back of my vehicle."

What a tough question for a stubborn goose like Gilda. She did not like to accept help, and she still held a grudge against Mrs. Pelican. On the other hand, she didn't want to miss Jenny's wedding.

"Oh, all right," replied Gilda. "I'll ride with you, but only if you let me pay for gas."

"Of course," said Mrs. Pelican. "I will enjoy your company on the long drive."

Then Mrs. Pelican said, "Would you please check the map there on the seat and tell me where I should turn up ahead?"

Gilda said, "Eenie, meenie, miney, moe" and told Mrs. Pelican to take I-65 North. However it was clear ten minutes later when they got to the Ohio River Bridge that they were headed in the wrong direction.

Gilda thought, "I don't want to miss Jenny's wedding. I guess I better use the map and get us back on track." So Gilda checked the map and told Mrs. Pelican to turn around and take I-65 South toward Nashville. She checked the map again in Nashville and told Mrs. Pelican to head toward Chattanooga.

As it got darker, Gilda had more and more trouble reading the map and road signs with her dark goggles on. They almost missed an exit to Atlanta out of Chattanooga, Tennessee. With the black goggles on,

Atlanta looked like *Arizona* to Gilda, and they weren't going to Arizona. At the last minute, Gilda realized the sign said *Atlanta* and she told Mrs. Pelican to exit. They exited with a squeal of tires, and many cars honked at them as they cut across four lanes of traffic.

"Dear," said Mrs. Pelican, "why don't you take off those dark goggles so you can see the map and road signs better."

Gilda hated to be told what to do and almost honked, "No!" without thinking. But she counted to ten while she stretched out her long neck. "I'll compromise," she honked. "I won't take off the goggles, but I will take off the black film. After all, it is just a protective covering."

"That's good, dear," said Mrs. Pelican. "I believe we will get to Florida more quickly if you can clearly see the map and the road signs."

So Gilda took the black film off her goggles and was a splendid guide for the rest of the trip. Mrs. Pelican and Gilda arrived safe and sound (and right on time) for Jenny's wedding in Florida the next day. They had a great time, listening to marimba players, dancing the salsa (a very fun dance), and eating dozens of little smelt (a type of fish) until they fell asleep to the sound of ocean waves gently lapping at the shore. Soon it was time to drive back home.

During the ride back home, they talked and honked and one thing led to another. Gilda told Mrs. Pelican she had never learned to read. Mrs. Pelican said in a kind voice, "I always worried about you, Gilda, and always wished that I had offered to tutor you myself."

Deep down inside, Gilda knew that it was her own fault she had never learned to read.

"Mrs. Pelican," said Gilda, "that was so long ago. Any silly goose could have learned to read in ten years. It's not your fault at all. I should have done my homework, and I shouldn't have dropped out of tutoring or school."

Gilda may ride a motorcycle and go waterskiing with her friends at Lake Patoka, but at least she doesn't date milk cows like her cousin Henrietta or play volleyball with her long beak and puncture the ball like Sammy Stork. And after that memorable trip to Florida, Gilda stopped blaming others for things that were within her control.

Gilda decided that Mrs. Pelican was a pretty good old bird after all. As a matter of fact, she cooked bouillabaisse (a delicious fish stew) for Mrs. Pelican every Friday night, and in return, Mrs. Pelican tutored Gilda in reading twice a week. Now, Gilda reads to her in the car when they drive together to Florida every year to visit Jenny.

So if you ever see an old pelican and a young goose riding together on a black motorcycle on some dusty country road in rural Kentucky, tell them I said, "Hi," and, whatever you do, please try not to stare.

THE BOTTOM LINE: No more blame game!

Treatment Interventions

Give Up the Game

Discuss ways in which people don't take responsibility for actions:

Language
- Passive tense instead of active. "I'm sorry the chair fell on your leg." As opposed to, "I'm sorry. I backed into the chair so hard that I tipped it over on you. I didn't mean to hurt you."
- Using "you" instead of "I" statements. "You make me so mad." Instead of "I get frustrated and angry when you disobey me."

Excuses
- "I couldn't get up to take her to school—I was up all night with the baby."
- "He doesn't know any better—he was raised that way."

Denial
- "The fighting didn't hurt them—I made sure they went to another room when we were fighting."
- "He was grown up for his age and took good care of the other kids—no one got hurt."

Rationalization (Give Reasons Why)
- "I don't want to stop them from seeing their father—kids need their father in their life, even if he drinks."
- "He (abusive partner) can't help what he does. He was abused as a kid."

Project Blame
- "If you hadn't been standing there the chair wouldn't have hit you on the leg when it fell."
- "If you had told me you were afraid, I would have left him (abusive partner) sooner!"

1. Therapist asks each family member to think of a time he or she made a mistake but excused it, denied it, rationalized, or blamed someone else.
2. Each person writes down the situation and two ways of handling it—one the negative way and one in which the person takes responsibility.
3. Read the examples one at a time and discuss the choices.

4. Each family member describes a time he or she felt unfairly blamed by someone else. Did the person use language, denial, excuses, blame, or rationalization?

Take-It-Home Discussion Questions

Therapist may assign one or more of the following questions for the child to answer and discuss with parent, foster parent, or staff or prior to the next session.

Have I ever acted stubborn like Gilda?
Do I ever hate to ask for help?
Do I blame other people for my mistakes?
Did I ever blame someone for something that was my fault?
Did I ever dislike someone who later I came to like or respect?
What is something I had to change about myself in order to be success-
  ful?
Am I more like Gilda or more like Mrs. Pelican?
When am I most likely to blame others for my problems?

BLAMING THE VICTIM

In the next story, a "know-it-all" monkey criticizes a friend for falling in quicksand. Rather than providing support and assistance, he blames her for the accident. Not only does he blame her for falling in; he does not take advantage of opportunities to help her out. In his self-righteousness he is blind to her needs and lectures her about what she is doing wrong. The story is a nice "lead-in" to discussing ways that family members can better support one another rather than assigning blame or being critical of one another's efforts.

Families in treatment will chuckle at this story, recognizing similarities between the story's characters and themselves. As they use the story to discuss ways in which they might be less passive (take action), they can stop blaming others (treatment providers, friends or relatives, their children) and begin to "own" their choices and decisions.

FIRST THINGS FIRST

Once upon a time, three young spider monkeys were walking down a long, muddy path in the middle of the South American rainforest. Harry, Larry, and Mary were very tired from their busy day, and Harry was carrying a long rope. They had used the rope to play "Drop in the Lake." That is a game where monkeys take turns swinging out over the lake and then dropping into the cool refreshing water. Then the monkeys have to swim really fast back to shore before the hungry crocodiles catch them.

What fun the monkeys had that day at the lake! They played "Drop in the Lake" over and over until they started to shiver in the cool breeze that was blowing. The next thing they knew, all three monkeys were very hungry. "Let's go eat our picnic lunch," suggested Mary. So the three monkeys sat down under a banana tree and had a yummy picnic of bananas, honey, fresh green leaves, and termites.

Now, they were on their way home. Harry, Larry, and Mary were too tired to swing from tree to tree and decided to walk. It had rained hard for three days, which it often does in the rainforest, and there were many deep puddles along the way.

The monkeys tried leaping over the puddles but often did not make it.

Jump, plop, splash! Jump, plop, splash!

Now, in addition to being very tired, they were very muddy. As they came upon a particularly muddy section of the path, Mary tried to jump over the thick mud.

Jump, plop, GLUG! GLUG?

"Oh my!" thought Harry and Larry as they realized Mary had landed right in the middle of the mud. And, as they watched, Mary started sinking, right where she had landed. Soon the mud was up to her ankles. She pulled and tugged, but her feet would not come loose.

"Look there," said Harry to Larry. "Mary is sinking into the mud. I wonder if that is quicksand."

"It might be quicksand," said Larry. "Harry, why don't you just throw her the rope and pull her out?"

Harry, instead, went over to where Mary was stuck and looked down at the mud. He got down on his hands and feet, leaned over, put one hand into the mud, and felt around. No bottom. "Yup," he said to Larry. "It's quicksand."

By now Mary was calling out loudly, "Please help me! I'm sinking!" Mary had sunk down to her knees and was thrashing around wildly in the sucking, slurping quicksand, which gripped her tightly.

Larry said, "Harry, just throw her the rope and pull her out!"

Harry instead said, "Mary, if you keep thrashing you'll go in deeper. Don't you know that in quicksand you need to stay still and move slowly? The more you struggle, the faster you will sink."

Larry said, in a stern voice, "Harry, quit being such a know-it-all! Just throw her the rope and pull her out!"

But Harry liked being a know-it-all and said to Mary in a know-it-all voice, "Mary, if you lie on your back in the quicksand, your feet will come up and you can float until someone rescues you. That's what you need to do."

Mary did not know how to float, and now the thick mud was up to her neck. She was still sinking. Her face was tilted up, and she was trying hard to stay above the surface. Any minute now, she was going to sink below the surface of the quicksand.

Larry said in an insistent voice, "Harry, throw her the rope, NOW. This is not the time to give Mary a lecture. She needs your HELP!"

At this point Harry finally noticed that Mary was very red in the face and tilting up her face to keep her nose and mouth above the surface. "Maybe," he thought, "I should help Mary, since she is doing all the wrong things. She has sunk down so deep that nothing she does on her own will save her. I *could* throw her the rope and pull her out."

But at that last thought, Harry felt the rope suddenly jerked out of his hands. He watched as Larry raced over to the muddy quicksand and threw the rope to Mary, who was now gagging on the muddy water. She grabbed it with great relief. Mary leaned back as Larry tugged, and ever so slowly she floated up to the surface. As the suction broke, Larry gently pulled Mary back to hard ground.

"Whew!" said Larry. "That was a close call!" He gave Mary a big hug and turned to Harry with a frown of annoyance. "Harry," he said, "what were you thinking of? When someone in real trouble needs your help, you help first and talk later!"

Harry replied, "But I like to do things by the book. When you're right, you're right." (In case you did not know it, by the book means following the rules.)

Larry pointed out, "You have the right of way when the traffic light is green, but if you walk in front of a truck that is running the red light, it won't matter. You'll get killed. You would be *dead right* in that case."

"OK," said Harry, "I get the point. There are more important things than always being right." He turned to Mary and said, "I'm sorry I didn't throw you a rope. I was too busy giving advice and judging you. Please forgive me!"

"Oh Harry," said Mary, "of course I forgive you. Thanks to you, at least I know what to do the next time I get stuck in quicksand." She added, "I am very glad, though, that Larry was there to save me." Mary gave Larry a big hug of thanks.

Larry, Harry, and Mary continued on home. This time, Larry carried the rope. You never know when you might need a rope to help a friend in trouble.

THE BOTTOM LINE: First things first.

Treatment Interventions

A Helping Hand

1. Therapist asks each family member to draw a rope on a piece of paper.
2. On one end of the rope, family members write or draw a past or current situation where they would appreciate help.
3. Each family member passes his/her paper to the right. The next person writes something at the other end of the rope that he or she will do to help. This help can be listening, support, chores, hugs, etc.
4. Keep passing the papers until they return to their owners.
5. One at a time, read the situations and the offers of help.
6. Ask each family member to give an example of a time he or she needed help or support but got criticized, ignored, or judged instead.

Healing a Broken Heart

Remind the family members of the girl's broken heart from *The Girl with the Plastic Heart.* Suggest to them that if her family members had taken responsibility for their actions and words, her heart would have healed, and then she would not have needed a plastic heart.

1. Therapist gives each family member a large heart cut out of construction paper.
2. On the heart, using a permanent marker or glitter glue, a child writes something his/her parents did that broke his/her heart. Explain that hearts can be broken by fear, anger, shame, cruelty, cursing, rejection, abandonment, physical abuse, neglect, and sexual abuse.
3. The child talks about what he/she needs from the parent that will mend his/her broken heart.
4. Parent cuts out and labels a paper "Band-Aid" (a smaller rectangle of paper) with something he/she will do to help mend (heal) the child's broken heart—"love," "patience," "quiet voice," "hugs," "protect," etc.
5. Parent glues the Band-Aid on the heart and tells the child he/she is sorry.
6. Parent asks the child what he/she can do to protect the child's heart in the future.
7. The child tells the parent what the parent could do to protect the child's heart in the future.

Hamburger Hurter

Things go wrong in families, as they do a casserole. The finished product is not what it was meant to be if the wrong ingredients are used, if the casserole is not given enough time to bake, and when no one keeps an eye on it while it is baking.

1. Therapist asks the family to draw a family casserole, *Hamburger Hurter,* that didn't turn out as planned.
2. Therapist explains that the casserole is made up of ingredients. When you make a casserole, you need to use the right ingredients, mix it well, watch it while it is baking, take it out when it is done, etc.
3. Ask family members to work together to complete the "What Went Wrong in Our Casserole?" worksheet (page 146).
4. Therapist invites family to draw the casserole in a way that illustrates what went wrong in the family.
5. Therapist leads discussion about "What Went Wrong?" Did family members get sick from eating it? Who got sickest and took the longest to recover?
6. Therapist asks family members to answer this question: "What can I do to improve our family casserole?"
7. Put a casserole dish in the center of the family circle. Ask each family member to write down a couple of ingredients that are needed to make a healthy family casserole and put them in the dish. Read and discuss.

Telling the Child's Story: The Child's Point of View

This exercise will take several weeks and will help parents better understand abuse/neglect from the child's point of view. It is best done after the child's therapist has clarified the nature and circumstances of the abuse or neglect of the child. The activity has two parts: the *trauma narrative* and the *impact statement.*

Goal: The parent will write a narrative about what happened in the family that led to CPS involvement, from the child's point of view. The child will work on his or her own narrative in individual therapy. The parent will then write an impact statement about how the child was affected by the abuse or neglect.

Steps of the Trauma Narrative
1. The parent will write his or her child's narrative, in the child's voice. He or she will review it with a therapist or parent group before sharing it with the child.
2. When parent has finished child's story and cleared it through a therapist or parent group, he or she reads it to the child in therapy session. Child tells the parent if he or she "got it."
3. The child then shares his or her version of the story with the parent, one that he/she has worked on in individual therapy—child's version may be a comic book, drawing, metaphorical story, puppet play, etc.

Steps of the Impact Statement
1. The parent reviews a series of questions and discusses his or her answers to the questions in parent group or individual therapy.
2. Parent writes an impact statement, from the child's point of view.
3. An impact statement describes how the parent's abusive or neglectful behavior affected the child. It summarizes losses, the child's feelings, and ways the child's life has been changed.
4. The parent shares the impact statement with a therapist or parent group before sharing with the child in a family session.
5. The parent reads the impact statement to the child in session, and the child tells the parent if he/she "got it right."
6. The child's impact statement is largely done through the *Bear of a Different Color* interventions, the desert and oasis activities that arise from *Stick Together*, the "Mad List," and "Your Day in Court."

Trauma Narrative Parent Instructions: Telling My Child's Story
1. This assignment will help you understand your child's point of view about the choices you made and things you did or didn't do that led to your family's involvement with CPS.
2. Pretend to be your child. Tell your child's story from the child's point of view. To do this, put yourself in your child's "shoes" and use first person "I" sentences.
3. Before you write the narrative, ask yourself (honestly) what your behavior might look like to your child. Write your answers to the following questions and share the responses with your therapist.

   • Was your behavior frightening or mean?
   • How did you act like a kid/teenager instead of a grown adult or a parent?
   • What did you do or say that was intimidating or threatening?
   • What did you do or say that seemed lazy or uncaring?
   • What did you do that was not responsible?
   • How did you act when you got out of control?
   • How were your actions unpredictable?
   • How did you put your needs before your child's needs?
   • How did you put someone else first, instead of your child?
   • How were you selfish?
   • How did you avoid the truth or tell lies?
   • How did you blame others for what happened?
   • How did you make excuses for what happened?

4. Write a one-page narrative in your child's words about what happened in your home that led to CPS involvement. Please think about what

your child might say to the child's therapist, especially if your child usually agrees with you or says what you want to hear (possibly due to fear of harm, to please you, or to avoid punishment). This narrative is about your child's response to *your* behavior and choices—things you did and said (or things you didn't do) that hurt someone who loves you.

Examples of Narratives   (eight-year-old girl) "When I was six, we lived in Kentucky. One night my daddy came home late—he always stopped at the bar on his way home. Mommy was mad that Daddy was late and asked Daddy where he had been. Daddy looked mad and told me to go my room and "don't come out." I heard Daddy call Mommy a F'ing B; Mommy yelled back. There was loud noise. It was Daddy's gun going off. I heard Mommy scream. I wanted Mommy. I was really scared and almost wet my pants. The front door slammed. Then it got real quiet. After a long time, I came out of my room. Mommy was crying and told me to go back in my room. I hugged her and said I couldn't sleep. She let me sleep in her bed. I peed the bed that night, and Mommy said it was OK. That night Daddy didn't come back. The next day CPS came to my school and said a neighbor had called. I told them what happened and they took me to a foster home."

Or

(Ten-year-old boy) "I was a good big brother. I remember when I was seven, my mom had to go to work and our babysitter was late. My mom left me in charge and said the babysitter would be there soon. She didn't want to lose her job. The babysitter didn't show up that day. I changed my baby brother's diaper and made sure my other brother got on the school bus. I had to miss school. I didn't have my mom's phone number, but I was OK. I used the microwave to cook soup and had Fruit Loops for dessert. When my mom got home that night at 9 PM, she said I was a 'good boy' for putting the baby to bed. She was really mad at the babysitter. When I told my teacher why I missed school, she called CPS, and I got taken away. I don't know why they did that—I was a good big brother!"

Parent Impact Statement Instructions   Abuse changes children's thoughts, feelings, and behavior, just like it changed Lucky in *Lucky the Junkyard Dog*. Some children become strong and resilient, while others develop problems. Please reflect on and answer the following questions before writing your child's impact statement. Review your answers in group or individual therapy.

- How has my child changed in and outside our family?
- Does my child doubt my word or have trouble trusting me?
- Does my child have trouble trusting other people?

- Does my child have a hard time getting along with others (kids or adults)?
- Does my child worry more about safety (at night, tornadoes, being alone)?
- Is my child afraid of things?
- Does my child act older or younger than his or her age?
- Does my child have bowel or bladder accidents?
- Does my child have nightmares or trouble sleeping?
- Is my child more angry or aggressive?
- Does my child have trouble talking about certain things?

Parent Impact Statement Instructions   Write, in your child's voice, a two-page impact statement that includes your child's answers to the questions below. Title the statement, "How My (Mom's, Dad's, Stepdad's, etc.) Behavior and Decisions Hurt Me." Review the statement with individual or group therapist and then share it with your child in family session. Your child will tell you if you "got it," so be as accurate as you can. Be prepared to correct it after sharing it with your child.

- What did I think about after I got removed from my home?
- How did I feel after I got removed from my home?
- What did I have to leave behind when I got removed?
- What did I lose in my old life?
- How is my new life different than my old life?
- How often do I feel sad?
- How often do I feel mad?
- How well am I sleeping at night? Am I having any bad dreams?
- What do I worry about from the past?
- What do I worry about that might happen?
- Am I more hyper than I used to be?
- Do I get in trouble for touching other children?
- How often do I lose my temper (curse, yell, hit)?
- Do I have a hard time getting along with others at school?
- Do I poop or pee in my pants or anywhere else?
- Do I talk about hurting other people?

The Transformer

The metaphor of a transformer toy is very helpful at illustrating change. Most children are familiar with this type of toy and they understand that with a few twists and turns, the toy is "the same" but "not the same." This is a good family or group activity.

Therapist Instructions:

1. Design a transformer toy that stands for you, before and after the abuse/neglect. You can draw it first and then build it if you want to (clay, pipe cleaners, boxes, or Legos).
2. The first design/version of the transformer is how you were before the abuse.
3. The changed version of the transformer is how you changed after you were hurt or neglected.
4. Be sure to change the design and colors to show the changes that occurred in you as a result of the family problems.

Discuss the finished products and have the child share them in group or family session.

Take-It-Home Discussion Questions

Therapist may assign one or more of the following questions for the child to answer and discuss with parent, foster parent, or staff or prior to the next session.

How am I like each of the monkeys?
When I need help, do I tough it out or ask for help?
Why did Harry do what he did?
How did Mary feel when Harry didn't help?
How do I feel when I need help and don't get it? Give an example.
Are there times I don't help due to my own "blind spots"?
When did I get lectured or criticized at a time I wanted support?
In my family or circle of friends, is there anyone that reminds me of Mary, Harry, or Larry?

WHAT WENT WRONG IN OUR CASSEROLE?

Please check the boxes below to show what you think went wrong in your family casserole. In the right column, put something that will help the "family casserole."

What went wrong?

- ☐ Someone changed the recipe (added or left out ingredients)
- ☐ Someone didn't bake it long enough
- ☐ Someone was in a hurry and made a mistake
- ☐ Someone forgot about it—it burned
- ☐ Someone fell asleep while it was baking
- ☐ Someone stirred the batter too long
- ☐ Someone left lumps in it
- ☐ Someone didn't pay attention to what they were doing
- ☐ Someone lost the cookbook or didn't use it
- ☐ Someone thought the cookbook was wrong and did it their own way
- ☐ Someone baked it in the wrong pan
- ☐ Someone set the oven too high
- ☐ Someone took it out of the oven without a potholder and dropped it
- ☐ Someone left it out on the counter and the dog ate it
- ☐ Someone ran out of supplies and substituted ingredients
- ☐ Someone used frozen ingredients
- ☐ Someone left the children in charge of cooking dinner
- ☐ Someone tried to bake it in the microwave

Something to make it better?

_____

_____

_____

_____

_____

_____

_____

_____

_____

_____

_____

_____

_____

_____

_____

_____

_____

_____

11

Safety and Protection

The stories and activities in this chapter help families consider risk factors and precautions they must take to ensure family member safety. Once families discharge from treatment, relapse risk goes up and sometimes parents or siblings don't recognize the risks present in their families, schools, and neighborhoods.

Children can be naïve and trusting, and it is up to parents to recognize safe and unsafe situations. It is important that parents not give too much or too little freedom. One will set children adrift to make their own decisions without adult input, and the other will lead to a lack of self-efficacy and limited coping skills. Some parents may have trouble understanding that who the adults choose as friends, i.e., those that are welcome in their home, additionally impacts their children's well-being.

Families in the process of reunification must have clear, detailed safety plans. Children also need to recognize unsafe situations and know how to use coping skills or access help when needed. They need a "backup plan" for times the adults in their world are not adequately protective.

"Relapse-prevention" talk takes place throughout treatment, in that the family members must understand what went wrong, anticipate risks for the future, and have a clear plan for avoiding risks and dealing with new situations that may arise. Parents may *have blinders on* about risks or may have unrealistic views of the amount of freedom that children can handle at different developmental stages.

It is easier said than done to get children and families to *follow* safety plans. Many parents remain blind to potential risk; and children will not follow safety plans if their parents don't enforce them. Modeling, coaching, and practice are necessary for families to create new life practices and eliminate old ones. Cultural factors must be considered as well, since what is viewed as normal by the family may not be legal or safe where the family is living.

Some parents are unable or unwilling to see the connection between their parenting behaviors and their children's problems. They view the safety plan as an externally imposed set of rules and do not realize the extent to which their behavior has an impact. In homes where a sexually reactive or highly aggressive sibling will be living in proximity to other children, a carefully prepared safety plan is imperative. Parents must learn to safely supervise sexually reactive and physically aggressive children.

Through therapeutic activities, family members become more comfortable with boundaries and limit setting, and risk will be reduced.

Regardless of whether children are reunified with their parents, they must learn coping strategies to build self-efficacy and feel safe in their daily lives. The stories and activities in this chapter help families talk more openly with one another about their own family risks and precautions they must take to ensure family member safety.

KNOWING WHO TO TRUST

The story that follows is about keeping a safe distance from predators and not being naïve about the risk that presents itself when they are around. The metaphors of meanness and hunger suggest that urges to hurt others can be nearly insatiable. It is clear in the story that a perpetrator needs firm boundaries and careful monitoring of his/her whereabouts. Through careful planning, the animals remain safe and avert attack.

It is difficult to begin discussion of one sibling's sexually reactive behavior toward another sibling. Therapists themselves can be overly "trusting" of potentially dangerous children or teens. They can teach families to accept the perpetrating sibling by loving him or her and displaying kindness while also setting firm limits on proximity and sibling behavior. They need to keep their eyes open to risks and hold siblings responsible for following the safety plan.

THE HUNGRY ALLIGATOR AND THE MEAN SNAKE

A group of friends were walking through the muck of a Florida swamp one sunny day in June when they heard a most horrific sound. "HSSSSSS," was the sound. Do you know what makes that sound? I hate to say it was not a teakettle boiling on the stove. "HSSSSS," came the sound again. Slithering their way was an ugly, mean-looking, bright green snake with a huge mouth and two big fangs sticking out of his mouth like a pair of buckteeth. With him was a nasty-looking, bumpy-snouted, long-tailed alligator.

"Hello, neighborsssssssss," hissed the snake with a sly smile, when he was about 20 feet away.

Kanga Kangaroo called out to her small friends, Madeleine Monkey and Mike Manatee, "Oh me, oh my, I don't have room for the two of you inside my pouch. Quick, get behind me!" You may be surprised to hear that a kangaroo, monkey, and manatee were hanging out together in a Florida swamp. Well, Kanga and Madeleine had escaped for the afternoon from a nearby zoo, and their friend Mike lived in a small cove in Smyrna Beach. Kanga had a baby kangaroo in her pouch, which was why she had no room for Madeleine or Mike at the present time!

"I'm in a bad mood," said the alligator.

"Me, too!" said the snake. "Let's go eat someone," he said.

"Yeah," said the alligator. "I feel like eating someone, too. I haven't had anything to eat for two weeks! And if I don't find anyone delectable enough to eat," he sneered, "I'm going to at least bite someone with my big, sharp teeth."

"Yessss!" hissed the snake. "I'd love to coil up and strike someone with my fangs." In case you do not know it, the word "delectable" means something very tasty or delicious.

Both the alligator and snake were in snappy, mean, sourpuss moods. It might have been because the snake had almost been turned into a snakeskin purse the week before, and the alligator had almost become someone's expensive alligator shoes. They had escaped with their lives in the nick of time when hunters had chased them through the Everglades, a large swamp in Florida.

The alligator and snake were also more hungry than usual. As the alligator had said, it had been two weeks since they had anything to eat. Because of the drought and the population explosion in Florida, there was not much food to be had for snakes and alligators. A drought is a long dry spell without rain; and a population explosion is when there are too many animals or people around and it is too crowded. Florida is definitely one place that is much too crowded, especially with alligators, snakes, and older, retired people.

"Hello," said Kanga bravely to the snake and the alligator as they approached. "Don't come any closer," she said.

"Lunch," said the snake to the alligator in a quiet sneaky voice.

"Oh, goodie," said the alligator, licking his chops and creeping a few steps closer.

"No," said Kanga. "Please move back. It's not nice to eat your neighbors."

Kanga had been wise to put her young friends behind her and to ask the alligator and snake to move back. She knew that you should never let an alligator or a snake get too close. It is their nature to strike, even if they act nice, smile, and pretend to be your friend. You would be very foolish indeed to let an alligator or snake give you a hug or kiss. If you let a boa constrictor curl up around you, he might squeeze the life out of you before you even realized what was happening. If you let an alligator give you a back rub, he could take a bite out of you from behind and you would never see it coming. And you would be even more foolish to accept an invitation to go swimming with them or to meet them for dinner. Probably, you would *be* the dinner if you accepted *that* invitation.

Kanga whispered to Mike and Madeleine, "They haven't eaten in two weeks, so I think they are going to eat *us* if we don't get them some food!

Madeleine whispered back, "Yes, let's get some food for them to eat. Then they won't eat *us*. Alligators and snakes are much more agreeable when they are full. They are downright mean when they are hungry!"

Kanga told the alligator and snake, "We don't really know what it feels like to be hungry. They feed us every day at the zoo, and we are well taken care of. Mike over there gets plenty of plants off the bottom of the cove. Why don't you let us go back to the zoo for some food for the two of you? Then you can eat until you are totally full."

"Alright," said snake and alligator. "We'll wait here with your friend Mike Manatee while you go get us some food, and if you're not back in 15 minutes, we'll eat your friend." That was a horrible thought for Kanga and Madeleine. They knew that manatees are large, gentle animals that move quite slowly. Mike had no protection against the awful, hungry alligator and mean snake.

Madeleine and Kanga went quickly back to the zoo and begged for some food to give the alligator and the snake. Luckily, it was the end of the day, and the zoo snack bars had quite a bit of uneaten, leftover food. They collected the biggest pile of food that you have ever seen and returned to where the alligator and snake waited with Mike Manatee. Madeleine was pushing a wheelbarrow full of food, and Kanga's pouch overflowed with the bounty.

"Open your mouths," said Kanga. Each opened wide. The snake could only open the front of his mouth at his hinged jaw, but the alligator's open mouth was huge and long, with many sharp teeth. "You need to use more toothpaste," said Kanga to the alligator, "as even from 20 feet away, I can see that your teeth are quite yellow."

The alligator snapped at her with annoyance and she hopped back another step. Kanga said, "I hope you'll be in a better mood after you have something to eat."

So Madeleine and Kanga began throwing them food. They used a slingshot to propel the food 25 feet, to keep the alligator and snake at a safe distance.

First, Madeleine tossed them five hamburgers, eight slushies, and three bags of popcorn. Next, six hotdogs, three chicken nuggets, two ice cream bars, and seven snow cones from the snack bar flew their way.

"Snap!" went the alligator's mouth.

"Yesssss!" said the snake. Soon all the food had disappeared.

"We're still hungry!" shouted the snake and alligator. "Give us more food, or we're going to eat your friend!"

"OK," said Kanga. She reached inside her pouch and pulled out ten bags of salted peanuts, two servings of nachos with peppers, ten cheeseburgers, and five ice cream cones. After a mighty pull on the slingshot, Kanga let go and slung the last of the food to the alligator and snake.

The not-quite-as-hungry alligator and snake gobbled it all down. As the last cheeseburger and ice cream cone disappeared, two loud burps sounded: "URRPPPP!" "URRPPPP!"

"Please say, 'Excuse me,'" said Kanga sternly, "and then say, 'Thank you!'"

The now quite agreeable alligator and snake each said, "Excuse me!" and "Thank you" as they reported that they were quite full. They were so full that they returned to the Everglades swamp to take a long afternoon nap and did not try to eat Mike Manatee or his friends.

Kanga and Madeleine said good-bye to Mike and went back to the zoo to eat lunch and take a long nap. Sometimes you need to take a nap after such a scary adventure.

You may find this story helpful the next time you come across a hungry alligator or a mean snake. First, get help right away and do whatever you need to do to remain safe. You might try feeding them, from 25 feet away, in case they are very hungry. But if that does not work, I recommend that you offer them a safe place to stay, like a cage or zoo! For when an alligator says to a snake, "Let's have our friends over for dinner," he means exactly that!

THE BOTTOM LINE: Do what you need to do to stay safe!

Treatment Interventions

Safe and Sound

This activity allows the family to "play out" safety themes, especially when a perpetrating family member is preparing to reunify with the rest of the family.

1. Therapist asks the children to choose an animal or puppet in the play therapy room that has hurt others in the past (alligator, snake, dragon, etc.).
2. Therapist asks the children to describe and demonstrate ways that the character hurts others by being "abusive" or "mean."
3. Therapist provides Legos and suggests that the family might want to create a safe cage/enclosure for the character. Therapist reminds family to make it a nice place, with food, water, and sunlight. This activity is a metaphor for the respectful boundaries that are needed with perpetrators. It also provides a metaphor for safely containing one's angry impulses.
4. Therapist reminds family members to allow the character out of the enclosure only at times when they can keep one another safe, even if the character promises not to hurt anyone. Remind family members that the character needs to show in behavior over time that he/she is trustworthy.
5. Therapist gives permission for the character to come out for five minutes and to remain appropriate. The character soon tries to bite or hit. Therapist, as the therapist, suggests that the child give character a time-out and helps the child carry it out.
6. After the time-out, the character continues to threaten others. The character, at therapist direction, is once again placed inside the safe enclosure. Therapist asks the family members to tell the character why it has been returned to the enclosure.
7. The character begs to come out and play; to sleep with the victim; promises to be nice; etc. Individualize the character to the family's situation. Ask family members to respond.
8. Therapist, as therapist, reminds the children that it is up to the adults to keep the children safe at the zoo.
9. Therapist reminds family members and the perpetrator that the character may act nice and even intend to keep his/her promises, but that he/she could be tempted to go back to old habits.
10. Therapist tells the family they must keep the character in the enclosure for now. They may feed him and talk to him, but they can't let him out.

11. Therapist reminds family members to keep a safe distance, i.e., not to get too close to the alligator due to the danger.
12. Therapist suggests that perhaps at some point in the future, the character can come outside the enclosure, but not until he or she gets used to being around the other family members and can be trusted.
13. Therapist asks family members what the character will have to do to earn the right to come back out and for how long.

Who's Who?

Therapist asks the family to decide who in the family would play each character in the story, including Kanga, Mike Manatee, Madeleine Monkey, Alligator, and Snake, and why.

Red Light, Green Light

1. Therapist talks with the family about red light, yellow light, and green light touch. Therapist compares this to traffic lights where the color determines whether we *stop, slow down and exercise caution,* or *move forward.*
2. This therapist does not use the words "good" or "bad" touch, since later in life, touch now called "bad" will be age-appropriate and acceptable. The focus of touch talk is on privacy and personal boundaries, not on moral labeling.
3. Red light is touch that is not allowed by anyone but the person, a parent putting on medicine or washing the child, or a doctor. It refers to private, hands-off body areas such as bathing suit areas. Red light touch often makes the other person embarrassed or uncomfortable. Red light touch would usually stop if someone else came into the room.
4. Yellow light is in the middle—it might be OK but it could move into red touch. For example, a back rub might be OK but if the hands started stroking in intimate ways, it would feel uncomfortable.
5. Green light is OK and includes comfortable types of touching.
6. Therapist asks family members to draw the outline of a large traffic light on a piece of paper. Therapist then provides construction paper in red, yellow, and green for family members to cut out three large circles.
7. Therapist asks family members to come up with as many examples of touching that fall into each color category (red, yellow, green) as they can in the next ten minutes and write them on the appropriate colored construction paper circle. Set the timer and say, "Go."

8. Family members glue their colored circles on the outline of the traffic light.
9. Therapist asks family members to give examples of times they have used or experienced the touch types on the traffic light. Start with green, moving then to yellow and red.
10. Family takes the finished traffic light home to display.

DOs and DON'Ts: Family Rules

Families must develop, with the input of the children, a set of family safety rules and identify what will happen if the rules are violated.

1. Therapist asks family to come up with rules about boundaries, touch, and family member interactions. Therapist provides family with a large piece of paper that is divided into two columns, "don't" and "do" rules.
2. Therapist asks that for every "don't" rule, the family adds a parallel "do" rule.
3. Go around the room, one at a time, each person suggesting a rule and the family voting to keep it or not.
4. Keep going until no one can think of anything else.
5. Therapist can interject some rules if they aren't suggested by the family (e.g., no bathing together).
6. Encourage family members to talk about what will happen if a rule is broken.
7. Therapist leads the family in a ritual where each person vows to support the rules and help one another to keep the rules.
8. Family members sign the rules, and post the rules in their home.

A Day Away from the Zoo

This is an appropriate activity for the reunification phase, when a perpetrator is re-entering the family. This activity revisits the zoo metaphor and shows that in time, the perpetrator can earn some supervised freedom and increased trust.

1. The alligator (played by therapist) asks the family to let him out of the zoo for the day and promises they can trust him now.
2. Therapist tells the family members to ask the alligator some questions about past behaviors and be sure they get honest answers.
3. Each person then asks the alligator why he/she should trust him/her now and what has changed.

4. The alligator must address each question. Others can help or coach him or her.
5. The family sets up rules about how and when the alligator can come out, what it is and isn't OK for him or her to do, and who will keep an eye on him or her.
6. The family unlocks the zoo gate and invites the alligator out, reminding him/her of the guidelines and family rules.
7. Alligator engages in appropriate and inappropriate behavior, and the family should respond accordingly.

Warning! Warning!

Families must become sensitive and responsive to potential risks. This activity teaches families and children about being watchful and protective.

Instructions: You have 30 minutes to create a magical, make-believe radar warning system. This system, when finished, will be very sensitive to things that are risks to children. You know, things that could lead to abuse, neglect, or harm.

- Your radar system will need to pick up on danger and sound some sort of alarm when risk or danger is present. When you need to sound the alarm, you will do that together as a group/family. Each family member will contribute his/her own sound effects. You will need to sound the alarm when you believe there is a risk present toward anyone in the family. Risk can be emotional, physical, or sexual.
- Give the family the Family Risk List (see page 157) to briefly review. Therapist then gives the family or group members some Legos, markers, glitter glue, wrapping paper, tape, cardboard, etc., to build and/or draw the make-believe radar system.
- Once the radar system is finished, Therapist asks each person to write down some low-, medium- and high-risk specific situations that could happen in a family. Some should be things that happened in their family.
- Therapist asks members to take turns reading risk situations. The group/family will sound their alarms if they think medium or high risk is present. Therapist provides input as needed.

Take-It-Home Discussion Questions

Therapist may assign one or more of the following questions for the child to answer and discuss with parent, foster parent, or staff or prior to the next session.

How do I act when I am hungry or lonely?

When the alligator or snake promises to be good, do I believe him?

What kinds of touches or physical contact are inappropriate?

How is a true friend different than an alligator or snake?

Have I ever trusted someone that was a "snake in the grass"?

Have I ever been a "snake in the grass"?

Have I ever done something that risked my own or my children's safety?

Am I still "hungry" to be "fed"?

What satisfies me when I am feeling annoyed, lonely, or fearful?

What do I "feed" myself when I am lonely?

How do I know when to trust someone? What are the signs of a true friend?

FAMILY RISK LIST

Inappropriate touching

Other behaviors that could lead to inappropriate touching

Threats of abuse

Exposing children to pornography, aggressive movies, adult materials

Asking child to break the law

Physical aggression or threats of aggression

Unsupervised Internet use

Poor boundaries (often around bathing, sleeping, dressing, privacy)

Unsafe situation (involves poor judgment on the adult's part)

Letting children go places where they could get hurt

Letting children do things where they could get hurt

Letting children spend time with people who could hurt them

Insufficient supervision

Letting children do things that aren't age-appropriate

Sleeping while children are awake, leaving young children alone

Taking care of children while under the influence of drugs or alcohol

Giving drugs or alcohol to children

Not supervising sexually reactive children

Not supervising aggressive children

12

The Family Journey

Pathways to Change

The "journey" of family reunification can range from months to years. When children re-enter the home, relationships and trust have to be re-established. Sometimes the children have changed (developmentally or emotionally) from those "frozen" in memory by the parents. Early in treatment, a therapist can introduce the concept of the family journey, suggesting that family members talk about and learn from the past; let go of the past; and move forward on new pathways.

Families move through the stages of Prochaska and Velicer's (1997) transtheoretical model of change (pre-contemplation, contemplation, preparation, action, and maintenance) at different rates. Some parents enter court-ordered treatment in pre-contemplation or contemplation, while others are further along the continuum. This model is an excellent one to use with parents, to help them understand that change is a process and that it takes time. The therapist may help them identify where within the continuum they lie when they begin treatment and how to tell when they have moved to a new stage.

Research suggests that therapists can help families move through the stages and recognize small changes in both attitude and behavior, since changes in thinking often occur prior to behavior change. Cognitive restructuring is needed to help parents move toward action, and irrational beliefs and family myths can be addressed so that they are not barriers to change.

Family members need non-threatening ways to talk about the past, and by using stories and hands-on expressive activities, they will be less defensive as they examine their past mistakes. As they discuss their dreams for the future and learn new ways to be parents, they begin to accept that treatment is an opportunity to change their relationships, their attitudes, and their behavior patterns.

Young children have cognitive and verbal limitations, but they can "talk about" the past (their understanding of what happened) using art, stories, dollhouse play, puppets, and/or drawings. What they draw or play out is often the "gist" of what happened to them (the main events, with strong sensory components). Children, especially those that were abused in pre-school years, often recall and process abuse through touch, sound, color, image, and kinesthetic modalities.

MOVING IN A NEW DIRECTION

As families move through treatment, they come to understand that change sometimes requires a move in a new direction. *Gold in the Desert*, the next story, allows families to consider how they have been *stuck* doing things over and over that do not work. The story ends with the suggestion that the main character may need to move in a new direction to achieve his goals.

After reading this story and discussing it together, we encourage families to create a mural of their family journey, and we start the mural in the first or second family session. The family journey may be depicted using a meta-phor of the family's choice, such as a trip down a long river with rapids, white water, calm waters, and dry low-water areas. Families may walk the Appalachian Trail, a rugged hiking path that goes many hundreds of miles through the wilderness. Or a family may take a trek in the desert, trying to find an oasis in order to survive.

It is useful to spend several family sessions creating the family mural. This encourages family members to take time to contemplate the past and commit to the change process (Prochaska & Velicer 1997).

GOLD IN THE DESERT

Once upon a time, a girl was taking a walk in the desert, just down the road from her house. Have you ever seen a desert? A desert is dry, bare, and flat as far as the eye can see. The hot sun glared down from high in the sky. Everything was dusty, and fine grains of sand kept getting into the girl's shoes. The heat made waves in the hazy, hot air, and off in the distance you could see the faint outline of a range of tall, snow-topped mountains. No one lived near the girl—her house was "out in the middle of nowhere" according to her friends.

As the girl walked, she took a drink from her water bottle and put some more sunscreen on her face and arms. Then suddenly the girl heard a loud voice: "Oh, CRAP!" The voice came from a tall man who was kneeling in the sand a few feet in front of her. Sweat was pouring down his red face as he scooped up some sand and sifted through it with a flat pan. The pan had very tiny holes in it and sand poured through them.

As the girl watched, the man threw down his sifter and said, again, very loudly, "Oh, CRAP!!!" The girl giggled to herself. Everyone knew that "CRAP" was a BAD WORD and not a nice thing to say. "I must be doing something wrong," said the red-faced man.

The girl was very curious and could not figure out what the man was doing. "Excuse me, mister," the girl said as she approached. "What are you trying to do?"

"That's obvious," he said. "I want to be a miner, and I'm searching for gold. I've sifted sand all day and haven't found ANY gold. I'm starting to get very upset. I've always been told that if you believe in yourself and work hard, you will be successful."

The girl thought, "He is one strange man! Everyone knows you sift for gold in a stream or mine gold up in the mountains. There is no water here, and the mountains are miles away."

The girl said, "I can tell that you have been working hard—your face is all red and you are covered in sand!"

Then the man said, "I feel like a failure, because I haven't found any gold. I must be doing something wrong."

The girl replied, trying to not hurt his feelings, "Mister, you're not doing anything wrong, but there is no gold here. Never has been—never will be. You might find gold up in the mountains. You're using the right tools—you're just looking in the wrong place."

"What do you mean?" asked the man.

"You could use that pan to sift through the sand in a stream up near the mountains," the girl answered. "If you want to find gold, you need to leave the desert."

"Oh darn," he replied. "I was afraid of that. I've always lived in the desert and don't really want to go anywhere else. I want to stay in the desert AND find gold."

"Mister," said the girl, "if you stay here, you're never going to find gold."

The man protested, "But what if I try my hardest, and pray night and day, and use my very best sifting technique?"

The girl said, "You're fooling yourself if you expect to find gold in the desert. There will never be any gold here. Even if you try your hardest, pray night and day, and use your very best sifting technique, you won't succeed."

"But as I told you before," replied the man, "I don't want to go anywhere else. I don't like to travel, and I'm very comfortable in the desert."

The girl said, "Sifting for gold in the desert is like trying to squeeze water out of a rock."

"You can't squeeze water out of a rock!" the man said.

The girl smiled playfully and handed him a small, hard, dry desert rock. "Go ahead and try," she said. "Squeeze it really hard." Just for fun, he gave the rock a squeeze. Of course, nothing came out of the rock.

She said, "Squeeze a little harder." So the man squeezed with all his might, but no water came out.

The girl teased, "Maybe you're not doing it right. Maybe you need to twist it or sit on it or rub it—surely if you keep trying, you will squeeze some water out of that rock?"

The man replied, "No, I can't squeeze water out of this rock."

"And why is that?" the girl asked.

He stated, "Because there is no water in it."

"Exactly," said the girl, "and there is no gold in that sand. Go to where the gold is if you want to find the gold."

The man realized that the girl was very wise for her young years. He could stay where he was (and quit hoping to find gold) or move on to a new place where gold was plentiful (the word plentiful means LOTS of gold). Just *knowing* he had a choice made a difference.

THE BOTTOM LINE: Go for the gold.

Treatment Interventions

Alphabet Journey

This is a good warm-up to play at the beginning of a family therapy or group session. The therapist should have a map and a feeling-words chart or list available.

Members will go through the alphabet, identifying places to which they will travel, what they will take with them for comfort, and what they will feel.

Using the alphabet, have family members (or group) go around the room and say, "I'm going to (A, B, C, etc., a place in the world) to find gold (identify what the gold or goal will be) and take along a (A, B, C, something for comfort or support). When I find my gold I will feel/won't feel (A, B, C, etc.) See how far you can get, with members helping one another out. If you can't think of a feeling for a certain letter of the alphabet, another feeling may be substituted.

Examples:

- I'm going to find gold (our family back together) in Alabama and take along my favorite Animal and then I won't feel Anxious.
- I'm going to find gold (my dad out of jail) at Birmingham, take along my Bear, and feel Better.

Water Out of a Rock

1. One at a time, therapist will ask group or family members to talk about something outside their control that they have been trying to change or control.
2. Therapist hands the first person the rock. Therapist asks, "What have you been trying to control or change that is not in your control and isn't working?" Therapist then asks that person to try to squeeze water out of the rock.
3. Model for group members by suggesting the person twist it, shake it, turn it, pound it, etc. Get them to join in. Suggest that the person is doing it "wrong" and needs to "try a little harder." Tell the person that he or she might want to squeeze a little longer.
4. When the person gives up and says he or she can't get water out of the rock, ask why. Agree with the person that there is no water in it. Then link it to the situation that the person has been trying to control. "You're right—you can't get water out of the rock; and you CAN'T do X either."
5. As the first person holds the rock, ask him or her to say what he or she might do instead. Then pass the rock to the next person. Keep going until each person has a turn.

The Family Journal Mural

This activity may begin early in treatment and continue across the treatment process. It gives families an opportunity to grieve the past as well as to develop clear plans for how they want things to change. It gives parents insight about how their actions have affected the children. Across several sessions, the family will create a series of murals to depict their family's journey. Therapist provides markers, glitter glue, magazines, scissors, felt or fabric, etc. in addition to a large paper roll. Note who takes the lead and have a discussion of the mural when it is finished.

#1: The Past   Instructions—Create together a family mural of your life's journey from X (past) until now.

1. Please include symbols that represent where you came from.
2. Each person is to include one thing you would like your family to leave behind from the past, and one thing you would like the family to keep and carry with you to the future.
3. You might want to use a river, garden, tree, road, or hiking trail or anything else to symbolize your journey.

#2: The Present   Instructions—Create a mural of your current life.

1. Include each family member.
2. Include extended family members that are involved in your lives.
3. Include friends or others that are part of your life now.
4. Each person is to include one thing you see as a family strength and one thing you see as a family barrier.
5. Each person is to include one of your own strengths and one thing you want to change.

#3: The Future   Instructions—Create a mural of where you want to go from here.

- Think about what you would like for your family in the future. What are your dreams? Where do you hope to be five years from now? Where do you imagine yourselves living?
- Include things you want in your future life that are not in your current life.
- Include one thing each of you wants to take with you from your current life and one thing each of you wants to leave behind.

Family Match Game

The Family Match Game asks the parent and child questions in a "game" format to see how well the parent knows and understands the child. Some of the questions are less personal and some more, and it is a safe "ice-breaker" in which children may share thoughts and feelings. It "challenges" parents to be accurate in order to earn points, but the point of the game is to increase parent understanding of the child's point of view. Use the Family Match Game worksheet found on page 166.

Take-It-Home Discussion Questions

Therapist may assign one or more of the following questions for the child to answer and discuss with parent, foster parent, or staff or prior to the next session.

How am I like the little girl?
How am I like the man?
Do I ever look for things in the wrong place?
Do I ever get stubborn and refuse to stop what I'm doing, even though it isn't working?
In my life, how am I "sifting sand"?
What is my "gold?" Draw a picture of it. What do I need to do to find it?
If I "go for the gold," what is the best thing that could happen? What is the worst thing?
How will I know I am ready to "go for the gold"?
What holds me back from moving in a new direction?
If I died today, what unfulfilled dreams would I have?
I am powerless to make someone else change. Is there anyone I have been trying to change?
When do I try to squeeze water out of a rock?

FAMILY MATCH GAME

Child's Name: _____

Parent Name: _____

Parents—play this game and see how well you know your children!
Children—play this game and see how well your parents know what you
think and feel!

Instructions:

1. Children take turns selecting questions to answer, one at a time.
   Past, then present, then future.
2. Child reads the question out loud.
3. Parent writes down the answer he or she thinks the child will give.
4. Child says his or her answer to the question.
5. Parent reads his or her answer.
6. You earn 5 points for each correct match! You lose 5 points for each
   incorrect answer.

The Past

What is your parent most sorry about doing or saying?
What is something your parent did that scared or worried you?
What is something your parent did that hurt your trust?
Describe an unfair decision your parent made.
What is your favorite family memory?
What is your funniest family memory?
What was your favorite Christmas while growing up?
What did you have the most fun doing together as a family?
What is your best memory from the past?
What is your worst memory from the past?
Who was your favorite teacher?

The Present

What do you like best about your parent?
What do you think is worst for a parent to do: yelling/cursing at a child,
   ignoring a child, or teasing a child in a mean way?
What does your parent like best about you?
What bugs you the most about your parent?
What do you do that bugs your parent the most?

What behavior do you most wish your parent would change?
What if anything does your parent do that hurts your feelings?
Who is your favorite relative?
How much do you trust your parent now? (1–5, 5 total trust)
On a scale from 1 to 5, how well does your parent discipline? (1–5)
Who is your favorite teacher?
Who is your best friend?
What is your favorite TV show?
What was your favorite movie of all time?
On a scale from 1 to 5, how much does your parent praise you?
What do you like doing the most with your parent?
What does your parent like doing the most with you?
Who is your favorite adult outside your family?
On a scale from 1–5, how well does your parent understand you?
What do you like least about how your parent disciplines you?
How fair are your parent's decisions? 1–5 scale.

The Future

How sure are you that you will never go back into foster care?
What two "old bad habits" do you think your family might return to in the future?
Where would you most want to live someday as a family?
Where would you most want to vacation or travel someday as a family?
Your family has made some changes. What 2 things do you hope your family will keep doing?
Your parent has made some changes. What 2 things do you hope your parent will keep doing?
Do you think your family will go back to their old ways after they leave treatment? Yes or no and why?

13

Coming to Terms with Out-of-Home Care

Some children are unable to be reunified with their parents (or siblings) due to high risk, parent pathology (alcohol, drug, mental illness), or parent incarceration. They may be placed in foster care, group homes, or other settings and need help to come to terms with living *in the system*.

Attachment is a biologically based drive, and children, even those abused and neglected, yearn to return home and to maintain a connection with their parents. But child protection is just that. Since children do not have the cognitive or emotional capacity to choose what is in their best interest, they need protection from harm.

Out-of-home care must be individualized, whether in a foster home, kinship care, or a group home. There need to be opportunities for free play and close adult-child relationships. Children need to develop secure attachments and experience a well-rounded, non-institutionalized life.

Good foster homes encourage affection and attachment while providing adequate structure. Unfortunately, some foster homes are too large, and the children do not receive enough one-on-one attention. Some foster parents favor their biological children or are judgmental toward their foster children, creating an us-them world.

A teen talked about an *us-them* living situation she had experienced in one of her foster homes. The home housed six foster girls and had two biological children. The foster children lived in the basement lower level of the home. One at a time, when they were *good*, the foster children were rewarded by being allowed to sleep upstairs. The *regular* family lived upstairs. The reason given was space, but the children had difficulty reconciling their feelings of being *less than* the family that had taken them in. Another girl always had to go to respite care when her foster family took a vacation or attended a special event such as an out-of-town wedding.

Some traumatized children are told to "grow up and act your age" when they display regressed behaviors. Some homes value compliance over autonomy, even though abused children need freedom to make some choices for themselves. They have known what it is to comply with controlling, abusive adults and will resist demands for compliance until they start to feel safe.

Group homes need to be as home-like as possible and provide children with positive, caring role models as well as access to formal treatment. Discipline should be positive, without harshness or negativity. The homes need to avoid staff turnover and encourage much family-like interaction. If routine and rules are valued over relationship, the children will not develop adequate relational coping skills. A "do it because I said so right now or else" attitude, or daring a child to cross a line in the sand, will lead to defiant line crossing every time.

It is up to therapists, foster parents, and staff to help children come to grips with termination of parental rights when it does not appear to be in the best interest of the children to return home.

OUT-OF-HOME PLACEMENT

Metaphorical stories and expressive activities help children realize they are not alone. After reading *The Good Enough Elf* story to siblings in foster care, one of the girls looked up at her therapist with disbelieving wonder in her eyes. "Do you know my mommy?" she asked. She continued, "You must know my mommy because that story is just like our family."

Adults who were raised in less-than-ideal foster home situations carry around feelings of anger, regret, and unresolved grief and loss that emerge years later. One fifty-something male client, socially and cognitively limited, bitterly *hated* his mother for leaving him due to her alcoholism and resented his father for placing him in foster care. "I was just trash," he often anguished. "They threw me away like trash. I'll never forgive my mother—she left all of us with my dad and drank her life away." His foster home experience had not been abusive nor had it been nurturing. "All I wanted," he added, "was someone to read me a bedtime story, tuck me in, and tell me I was a good boy." The story of *The Good Enough Elf* was written for this client.

The day the therapist read the story of the elf, the client moved to a beanbag chair on the floor, and the therapist tucked a blanket around him. As the therapist read to him, he closed his eyes and moved into a trancelike state. As the story ended, he said, "That's a lot like me!"

The therapist invited him to talk about when he was little and how he ended up in foster care. He spoke at length about his childhood experiences, sounding very much like a little boy.

The client then sheepishly said that he often felt like a little boy and became bitter and demanding toward others. The therapist suggested that when he felt like the "little boy," he could nurture himself. She showed him how to give himself a hug, and at that, he wrapped his arms around himself, snuggled into the blanket and beanbag, and got a sweet grin on his face.

"That's right," said the therapist. "You are a good boy and a good man, and you can remind yourself of that when you feel lonely or sad. Be good to yourself."

That session was a turning point for this man. Over the course of several months, he began to forgive his mother and began to see that her own problems had limited her parenting—it was not his fault. He developed more confidence in himself, reduced his angry outbursts, and made new friends in his day program.

There is never a "wrong time" to help clients resolve feelings associated with out-of-home care. Sooner is better, but it is never too late. *The Good Enough Elf* affirms that everyone is lovable, and that sometimes loving means letting go.

THE GOOD ENOUGH ELF (dedicated to H)

Once upon a time, there was a young green elf named Ella that was going to have a baby. Ella Elf had fallen in love with the baby's father. He drank too much elf nectar, though, and when Ella told him about the baby, he left her. He didn't want to be a father; in fact now he had his eye on a pretty fairy girl in the next town.

Ella's life had been very hard. Growing up, her mother told her, over and over, "You are good for nothing." Of course it was not true. But Ella believed what her mother said and blamed herself for her mother's bad moods. She was not really sure why her mother said she was "good for nothing." Ella thought maybe it was because she talked too much, or didn't listen, or had the wrong friends, or got bad grades in school.

When Ella told her mother she was going to have a baby her mother said, "See, I told you that you are good for nothing!" and kicked her out of the house. Ella got a job and rented a nearby apartment. She was alone in the world.

Soon Ella knew it was "her time" and got an elf midwife to help her deliver the baby at home. (In case you did not know it, "deliver" means to help the baby be born and a "midwife" is someone that helps the baby get born.)

"Congratulations," said the elf midwife. "It's a boy."

As Ella looked at her new baby and held him in her arms she said, "I love you, little elf. I want you to have a better life than I did!" But caring for a baby was not easy, and Ella was tired all the time. He cried a lot, as newborns often do. Once he cried all night, and nothing Ella did seemed to help. "I'm a bad mother," Ella thought.

The next week, her landlord came to collect the overdue rent. Ella Elf had used the last of her money to buy formula and diapers for the baby. "GET OUT!" said the landlord.

That night, Ella thought, "My son deserves a better life than the one I can give him." She cradled her darling baby and said, with tears in her eyes, "I want you to grow up happy and have the things you need."

Then Ella packed a small diaper bag and wrapped her baby in a warm blanket. With her baby in her arms, she walked until she came to a cozy-looking house on a tree-lined lane. A nice troll family with six children lived there, and they always seemed so happy. After looking to see that no one was watching her, she went up to the front door. "My little love," she said, "I'm sure the troll family will take good care of you and come to love you the way I do."

With that, she laid him gently down on the doorstep and knocked loudly. Ella Elf waited behind a tree until a kind-looking troll came to the door. "What a darling baby elf!" she heard. "Where did you come from? Let me take you inside, out of the cold!" The troll picked up the baby, and the door closed. Ella sadly walked away. The next morning, the troll family called Elf Services and asked to keep the baby in their home since no one had come back to get him. Permission was granted.

The troll family took good care of the little green elf. Soon he was not a baby anymore—he grew up strong and healthy, and the trolls came to love him like one of their own. But with six troll children and the little elf, there wasn't much room or money. When they thought the little green elf wasn't listening, the troll parents sometimes talked in worried, hushed voices about all the bills and how crowded the house was. But the little elf was listening. So one night, while the troll family was sleeping, he ran away. He wasn't old enough to take care of himself, but he didn't want to be a burden.

Elf Services found the little elf living under a bridge with a group of gypsies (in case you did not know it, gypsies are colorful travelers that move from place to place) and placed him with a family of dwarfs. This family wasn't as nice as the troll family, and they made him sleep on a pile of straw in the barn. He did chores for the dwarfs from sunup to sunset, and they made fun of him. "You are so small! What big ears you have!" they teased. Again he decided to run away, because the teasing made him cry.

So one dark, cold night, the little green elf left the dwarf house when no one was looking. The moonlight guided his way through the woods. He was scared, because he heard all sorts of noises. "I hope nothing tries to eat me!" he worried. He didn't know where he should go. "I wonder," he sighed, "if I will ever find a place to belong."

What he really wanted more than anything in the world was to find his green elf mother and live with her again. He didn't remember his mother or why she had left him. There must have been a reason. He thought, "Something I did must have made her leave me. Maybe I cried too much or ate too much. Perhaps I didn't sleep enough." Of course, it had not been his fault that Ella Elf had given him up. He did not understand that she loved him and wanted a better life for him.

The elf longed to have a "real home." "Maybe," he thought, "if I found my mother I would finally be happy. I would know who I am and where I belong."

The little elf didn't know that his mother lived only 20 miles away. He also didn't know that she lived with a mean elf that hated children and drank too much elf beer. Ella wondered what had happened to the baby she had given up so long ago. She hoped he had a good life and had never forgotten him.

The little elf was so tired that he curled up under a huge pine tree and fell into a deep sleep. Finally it was morning, and the sun began to rise, filling the sky with beautiful colors. The little elf shivered in the cold as he awakened, and he was glad to see the light of day. He was thinking about what to do next when he heard a voice. "Little elf! What are you doing all alone in the woods?" It was a grownup red elf, ahead on the path. The little elf knew he should not talk to strangers, so he said, "Why do you care, and who are you?"

The red elf called out, "Don't worry—I won't hurt you. I live in the next village and am on my way to work." The red elf approached, then stopped suddenly and exclaimed, "Little elf, I know you! You look just like your mother Ella!"

"How did you know my mother?" asked the little elf.

The red elf replied, "I knew your mother years ago; in fact, I remember when you were born. Your mother loved you very much, but she was very young and did not have enough money for food or rent. She cared for you the best she could. When her landlord kicked her out, she left you with the trolls. I thought you still lived with them."

"First I lived with the trolls and then I lived with the dwarfs. Now, I have nowhere to live. All because my mother left me," said the little green elf in an angry voice.

"Yes," said the red elf, "she left you—with the hope that you would have a better life."

The little green elf said, with a tear in his eye, "Sometimes I think I hate her, because she left me."

The red elf replied, "I understand why you might feel angry."

"Yes," said the elf. "I am Mad with a capital *M*."

"I can see that you are Mad with a capital *M*," replied the red elf. "I wonder," said red elf, "if you also might be a little hurt or sad?"

"Maybe a little hurt and sad," said the little green elf. "It is hard to grow up without your mother."

"Yes," said his older friend. "It is hard to grow up without your mother—it is a great loss."

"Well," said the green elf, "even if I am hurt and sad, I will never forgive her. She didn't love me."

"I think you're wrong about that," replied the red elf. "Your mother loved you enough to give you a chance to have a safe and better life." The little green elf thought about what the red elf had said.

He said, "So if what you say is true, perhaps my mother loved me after all. I always wondered why she left me. Maybe someday I will find a way to forgive her." The little green elf then told the big red elf all the things that had happened in his life and why he was alone in the forest.

The red elf said, "You are too small to be out here alone. I bet you are hungry and tired. Why don't you come home with me? I can give you a good meal and a warm bed. And if you want to stay, you are welcome."

The little green elf asked, "Why can't you take me to my mother? You are very nice, but I have always wanted to be back with my mother."

The red elf replied sadly, "Your mother is not in a good place right now. She still has a hard life. Maybe someday you will see her again, but right now, that's not possible."

The little elf didn't understand why the red elf was willing to take care of him. "Why are you, a red elf, willing to give me a home? Green elves and red elves have had trouble getting along for years! What will your neighbors think?"

The red elf replied, "Your mother didn't care if I was red or green. She was my friend. And you are welcome in my home."

The little green elf decided to stay with the red elf, and they grew to really care about one another over time. The little green elf came to accept that his mother had loved him enough to want a better life for him. He sometimes dreamed of his mother and wished he could see her. Since that wasn't possible, living with the red elf was the next best thing.

THE BOTTOM LINE: Sometimes loving means letting go.

Treatment Interventions

The Send Off

1. Therapist asks child to draw and pack a suitcase for the elf—what the child thinks he will need in his new home.
2. The therapist helps the child write a letter to the little elf, providing support and encouragement.
3. The child, as the elf, writes a letter to the elf's mother. The elf tells her all the ways she would be proud of him now; he also explains why he misses her so much and what he hopes for the future.

Take-It-Home Discussion Questions

Therapist may assign one or more of the following questions for the child to answer and discuss with parent, foster parent, or staff or prior to the next session.

How am I like the elf? Who do I trust to take care of me?
Why did the elf want to live with his mother?
Why did the elf blame himself for his mother giving him up?
Why did the elf's mother blame herself?
What did the elf and his mother have in common? (How were they the same?)
Do I think the elf should go live with his mother?
When in my life have I felt abandoned or rejected? When did I feel unlovable?
Does this story remind me of anything that happened to me?
Is there someone in my life (past or present) that I hold a grudge against and need to forgive?

IMPACT OF NEGLECT

The Bruised Orchid was written after a failed attempt at family reunification. And yet, looking back, it was the failure of reunification that led the "orchid" child to begin to talk about her internalized fear, pain, and anger. For, as we know, "benign neglect" is never benign when it refers to children. "A" was a very attractive nine-year-old, enmeshed with her mother, whose most common response to how she felt about anything was, "I don't know." She had the unfortunate experience of being "the favored child" in her family due to her tendency to avoid conflict, remain silent in the midst of stress, and "shut down" when anxious. Her siblings were more vocal and behaviorally out of control, so they received the brunt of the abuse in the family. She suffered silently and witnessed their maltreatment. The story that follows is a good introduction to talking with children about the need for nurturing care and how the absence can be harmful to their well-being.

THE BRUISED ORCHID (dedicated to A)

An orchid plant sat on the windowsill, looking droopy and sad. All but one of her beautiful purple blossoms had dropped off, and her leaves looked yellowish brown. She used to have six healthy blooms, and her leaves used to be a rich deep green. What had happened?

It was a matter of touching and watering. People just couldn't keep their hands off her. Her purplish pink blooms were soft and delicate, and she looked almost like a silk plant. But she was not made of silk—she was real! She had asked people not to touch her, but they didn't listen because she was so pretty and delicate; her owner had even put up a sign saying, "Don't touch the delicate orchid." But people could not resist saying, "Is that plant real?" and then they touched her pretty blooms.

The orchid's owner was distracted and didn't keep her in a safe place, so everyone touched her as soon as they came into her owner's house. The owner's friend had suggested that the owner place the orchid in a safer, more private place. But the owner left the orchid right in the middle of the entranceway to the house.

The orchid's owner didn't feed or water her the way she needed. An orchid needs daily care and sunlight—just enough water to keep the leaves healthy and just enough sun to allow her to grow. If you over-water or under-water an orchid, the blossoms drop off or it gets root rot and dies. And if you don't give it enough sun, the leaves turn yellow.

The orchid liked being pretty and she liked being admired, but she didn't like being touched. She wondered why people thought it was OK to do that without her permission. And she wished her owner would take better care of her.

One day, the owner's friend came over and said, "I'm going to take that orchid home with me, or she will die. She needs to be protected from all the touching that goes on at your house. She also needs sunlight, food, and just the right amount of water. When she is better, I'll show you how to feed her and what she needs to stay healthy. This orchid is a lot more than a pretty thing to show off."

With the proper care, the orchid got better. She grew new dark green leaves and a long stalk appeared with new buds. That meant she would soon have new flower blossoms on the stalk.

The friend asked the owner, "Are you ready to take better care of her? I can bring her back and teach you what you need to know. But if you take her back, you need to love and protect her. Letting people touch her delicate blossoms will damage them!"

The owner thought she was ready to care properly for the orchid, once her friend showed her how. But within a week, she was letting other people touch the new blossoms, and she forgot to water and feed the orchid twice. She didn't mean to hurt it—it just was too much for her to manage and she wasn't very organized. The leaves were already starting to turn brown again.

In the end, the friend offered to take the orchid back to her home and said to the owner, "You can come visit her anytime you like, as long as you let me know when you're coming. But the orchid needs regular care, and I don't think you are going to be able to provide it. I know you want to, but it isn't working."

The owner didn't like giving up the beautiful orchid, but she agreed that she just wasn't ready or able to be an orchid grower. She knew that her friend would take good care of the orchid. When the first owner went to visit two weeks later, she could see new buds. The orchid had bloomed with three new purple blossoms, and the leaves were turning green again. The orchid sat in a private window in the home, with just enough light. It was out of reach of visitors so that no one could touch it. And her friend kept it just moist enough and well fed. It was obviously healing from its prior neglect—it was in a good home.

Perhaps in time the woman would be better able to care for a delicate plant. In the meantime, she got a fish tank and a couple of fish, because she knew how to feed fish, and with fish you didn't have to worry about others touching them. For now, that would be enough.

THE BOTTOM LINE: Know your own limits!

Treatment Interventions

Some parents, in spite of good intentions, do not adequately nurture or protect their children. When that happens, alternate care must sometimes be provided. This story addresses some of the issues involved in neglectful parenting.

Orchid Activity

Read the story together and look at a picture of an orchid online or in a book.

1. Research the care that an orchid needs to stay healthy.
2. Discuss the story from each point of view: the orchid, the owner, and the owner's friend. Role-play the parts or discuss one at a time. I am the orchid . . . I am the owner . . . I am the owner's friend.
3. How are their points of view different?
4. What care do children need to stay healthy?

Take-It-Home Discussion Questions

Therapist may assign one or more of the following questions for the child to answer and discuss with parent, foster parent, or staff or prior to the next session.

How am I like the owner's friend?
How am I like the orchid?
Why did the orchid lose her blossoms?
Do I think the orchid should go live with her owner or with the friend?
How am I like the orchid's owner?
Who do I trust to take care of me?
Does this story remind me of anything that happened to me?
Is there an area of my life that deserves more of my love or attention?
How am I going to take good care of myself (my appearance, my well-being)?

14

Self-Acceptance and Hope

Each individual in a family must find self-acceptance, decrease blame, and believe there is hope for a changed future. Children and parents must come up with narrative understanding about how things can and will be different. Family members must identify strengths and buy into basic beliefs about how people need to treat those they love.

Most parents come to realize that their choices regarding their children involved both omissions (things they didn't do that they should have done) and commissions (things they did that they should not have done). They are likely to feel some guilt about past choices, which may lead to regret and a desire to be a different type of parent.

But it is not guilt that leads to change. It is the growth of self-esteem and awareness of competencies that lead parents to change. Part of helping families change is eliminating barriers such as poverty, mental illness, lack of education, absence of transportation, and deficient social supports. Families that are unable to become self-sufficient and self-sustaining are less likely to reach their goals; and it is difficult to develop positive self-esteem and hope in a climate of perceived failure.

A crucial issue is how to help parents return to society and become self-sufficient following incarceration for such crimes as child abuse, prostitution, drug crime, or domestic violence. Some incarcerated women entered into criminal activity as a condition of their relationships, since they partnered with abusive men who engaged in drug or other illegal activity. Many women do not have the education, financial resources, or other means to live on their own, and they "repeat history" by entering into the same types of relationships as those in the homes in which they were raised. For example, there is a high rate of prior sex abuse in women arrested for prostitution.

Some women give birth in prison, and it is imperative that their babies have the opportunity to attach to them if they will be living with them later. Secure infant attachment will reduce the risk of later abuse or neglect. Mothers are often unable to obtain employment and housing post-incarceration—as a rule, many agencies will not hire felony offenders. And with a felony record, some individuals will be ineligible for social services such as food stamps. If states want to reduce crime and foster care placements, they need to ensure that women coming out of jail or prison have access to resources and treatment that will help them learn new parenting patterns and become self-sufficient.

Family treatment programs must utilize family strengths and celebrate even small successes. It is not our place to become judgmental toward families or to expect them to become "ideal" nurturing units. Agencies sometimes set "unspoken" goals for "optimal" parenting—you know, the ideal living situation where houses are perfectly clean, larders are full, meals include vegetables, no one curses or yells, no one drinks, and no one suffers from mental illness.

But "ideal" is not the goal. It makes it too easy for foster care and group home providers to "overprotect" children from "less than ideal," but "good enough" parenting. It is our professional responsibility to ensure that children are safe from abuse, attend school daily, and receive "good enough" parenting, so that families, whenever possible, might remain together.

LOWERING DEFENSES

In the story that follows, *Polly's Plight*, the main character is urged to strip off her protective defenses and find the beauty within. For years she had covered herself and her pain in layers of clothing and odd materials. Many years ago, I heard Bill O'Hanlon tell a client, "There is *nothing* about you that is unacceptable—take all the things you have put aside about yourself (the 'not me' parts), and bring them back." He also told a wonderful story, *A Wizard of Earthsea* (LeGuin 1968), about a young wizard that created a monster by accident and then spent all his time and energy running from the monster of his own making. The monster of his own making finally challenged him to quit running and hiding, and he decided he would kill the monster. In the end, the only solution that would free him was to drop his sword at the moment of conflict and embrace the monster. By embracing his worst "side," he made himself whole, and the monster was gone.

Polly is like the wizard. She avoided facing her pain and remained less than whole. By stripping off her defenses, she freed herself. That is the wish we have for our clients—to free themselves from the past by embracing it—only then will they find the capacity to become *more* than they were before.

POLLY'S PLIGHT

Someone was waiting on the sidewalk to cross the street. You will notice that I did not call the person "he" or "she." That is because you could not tell if it was a man or a woman. The person was covered from head to toe in a suit of armor, except for two dark eyes peering out of the opening over the face.

The light turned green, and the person stepped awkwardly off the curb, one stiff leg at a time. "Clunk, clunk, CLUNK!"

A little girl on the other side of the street tugged at her mother's sleeve. "Mom, look over there!" she cried out as she pointed to the armored person now sprawled on the pavement. "Let's go help!"

Her mother agreed, so they crossed the street after looking both ways for cars. The two of them approached the metal-covered person, who was clanking and rolling around, trying to get back up.

The girl looked down and said, "Can we help you up before a car hits you?"

"Thank you," said the person. "It's hard to move around in this armor, and I can't see where I am going."

So they each offered a hand and pulled the person to his or her feet. "*Buses, and taxis, and cars, oh my!*" exclaimed the girl in an excited, scared voice as the three of them walked arm in arm to the other side of the street.

"Just kidding," she said with a smile. "I always did like that scene from *The Wizard of Oz.*"

When they were nearly at the curb, the girl said, "Be careful now, and step up over the curb with your left foot."

"OK," said the person in armor, with a smile in his or her voice, as he or she stepped carefully up over the curb, one stiff leg at a time. "Clunk, clunk."

Once they were all up on the sidewalk, the girl asked, "What's your name?"

The person answered, "My name is Polly."

Then the little girl asked, "Isn't it awful warm in there?"

Polly replied, "Yes, but I'm used to it. I have worn this armor since I was a girl."

The girl asked some more questions. "Why do you wear it? What do you look like under the armor?"

The girl's mother stopped her. "Please leave Polly alone. You are asking too many questions."

Polly replied, again with a smile in her voice. "It's OK. I can answer your daughter's questions. I wear it for protection. I don't really know what I look like under the armor, since I've worn it for such a long time."

The little girl asked, "Protection from what?"

Polly replied, "I don't really know anymore. I used to need it. I guess I could take it off."

The girl said, "Let us help you. You'll be much more comfortable."

"OK," Poly agreed. So they all pulled and tugged on pieces of armor until a huge pile of metal was lying on the sidewalk.

"Oh my goodness!" exclaimed the girl as she stared at Polly in surprise. "Mom, look what Polly's wearing under the armor!"

Polly looked like a human cocoon, with layers and layers of fabric, tape, and other things wrapped around her. The outside layer, now that the armor was gone, was Velcro. It, of course, was very rough and prickly.

The girl said, "Polly, you are wearing Velcro and so many other layers under the armor. Why do you wear so many layers?"

Polly replied, "When I was about your age, something bad happened to me, and I wanted to cover up. The first layer was a furry coat—it made me feel safe at a bad time in my life. After that, whenever anything bad happened to me, I added a new layer." Polly added, "The layers protect me. If I fall down, I bounce back up. I can't scrape my elbows or knees. If someone hits me, I can't feel it."

The little girl then asked, ""What other layers do you have?"

Polly replied, "Let me think a minute so I don't get them out of order . . . "

Then she began,

"Layer #1 is a furry coat.

Layer #2 is a black leather jacket.

Layer #3 is a heavy-duty tin foil mummy wrap.

Layer #4 is duct tape.

Layer #5 is a hand-stitched quilt.

Layer #6 is a down jacket.

Layer #7 is an insulated black diver's suit.

Layer #8 is a lamb's wool cape.

Layer #9 is a sandpaper poncho."

She said, "I'm not sure about layers 10 and 11."

Polly added, "And as you can see, the top layer now, #12, is Velcro, prickly side out. Layer #13 was my suit of armor.

"You know," she said, "I added the armor when someone poked me with a barbeque skewer. I figured nothing could get through a suit of armor."

The girl commented, "I don't really see why you stay all covered up. You have protection from injury and pain—but you can't feel ANYTHING! You can't feel the sun on your skin or the rain on your face. If someone gave you a hug, you would never know it. And it must be very hard to ride a bicycle or walk up a hill."

Polly admitted, "It's true that I miss hugs, and I wish I could feel rain and sunshine on my face. But I'd rather be safe than sorry. My layers keep me safe."

The little girl asked, "How do you know you still need all those layers? Can't you take a few off? Just because you needed them before doesn't mean you need them now."

Polly wrinkled up her forehead and closed her eyes, thinking. Then, with her eyes wide open, she said, "Well I guess I could take off the Velcro and a few other layers. I might be able to move around better."

The girl and her mother said, "We can help." Polly lifted her arms up over her head, and they helped her take off the Velcro. As the last strip of Velcro came off, they saw Layer #11, a layer of soft red flannel, underneath.

"This is a real adventure," said Polly. "I forgot there was a soft flannel layer underneath the rough Velcro. Let's see what's next!"

Together they peeled off the flannel and then Layer #10, which turned out to be clingy cellophane. When they got down to Layer #9, the sandpaper poncho, Polly said good-bye to the girl and her mother.

"That's enough for one day," she announced. "I need to think about how many more layers to take off. Let's meet again tomorrow—3 o'clock at Pernicano's Pizza." The girl and her mother agreed and went on their way.

The next day their waitress came to the table and looked at Polly very strangely, probably because Polly was wearing the sandpaper Poncho.

"A large double cheese, double pepperoni and a pitcher of root beer," they said.

And then, while they waited for their pizza, the girl and her mother helped Polly peel off the rest of the layers, one by one. Polly kept exclaiming things like, "Ooh, that one's ugly!" or "Duct tape is so hard to take off in a restaurant!"

Layer by layer came off. Polly began to look less round and a little more human. Soon they could see a sweet smile, rosy cheeks, and dark eyes.

"You're very attractive," said the girl. "But you hid it well."

"That's OK," said Polly. "Until now it didn't matter."

At the furry coat, the last layer, Polly paused for a long time. She looked serious and sad. "I don't know if I can take this one off. It brings back bad memories."

The girl replied, "It's OK—you don't need it anymore. You don't need to hide *any* part of you."

Polly realized that the bad times had not changed *who* she was—they had changed how she saw herself.

And so Polly unbuttoned the furry coat, took it off, and dropped it to the ground. "Now I can finally see who you really are," said the little girl.

Just then, the waitress brought their large double cheese, double pepperoni pizza to the table. She put it down and sliced it with a metal wheel. "There's something different about you," she said to Polly as she tried to figure out what had changed.

"I can't figure it out," she said, "but whatever it is, it is a good change!"

Polly and the girl shared a smile, because they agreed with the waitress. It was a very good change, indeed.

THE BOTTOM LINE: Peel off one layer at a time!

Treatment Interventions

Peeling Your Onion Feelings

1. Show the family or group an uncut onion. Ask them what they will see if you cut the onion open.
2. Cut the onion in half and show the family or group the layers.
3. Explain that feelings are like the onion—they are layered. Point out that anger is an "on top" feeling and that other deeper, hard-to-express feelings often are underneath anger.
4. Discuss some of the feelings that can be hidden by anger: sadness, guilt, pride, hurt, embarrassment, self-blame, fear, anxiety, depression, failure, shame.
5. Explain that self-disclosure is like peeling an onion—very personal things lie deep inside and are harder to share. It usually takes trust to share deeper feelings.
6. Ask members to share at least one example of a time when anger covered up a deeper feeling, when they hid a feeling from others.
7. Photocopy and hand out the "onion" worksheet (page 188) and the list of feeling words (page 189). Ask family members to write the names of the feelings they find hardest to show or express at the core and those easiest to express at the surface (the outer layers).

Peeling Away Memories

Hand out another copy of the onion worksheet. Ask family members to write some memories from their lives, including some from childhood and teen years, on the onion. Put the toughest memories to talk about at the core and easier memories on the outside. Discuss.

The Family Cake

This is an excellent metaphor to help family or group members identify the ingredients of a healthy, safe, happy family.

1. Therapist instructs that each member is to draw a "healthy family" cake and include the necessary ingredients for becoming a healthy family. They should include ingredients necessary for a safe and loving home.
2. Therapist instructs each family member to draw and label what he/she considers to be "icing on the cake."
3. Discuss each picture. What are the necessary ingredients?
4. Invite family members to answer the question, "How is this cake different than our family in the past? Now?"
5. Invite the family members to say what ingredients they need to add or leave out in order to have a better tasting cake.

THE "ONION" WORKSHEET

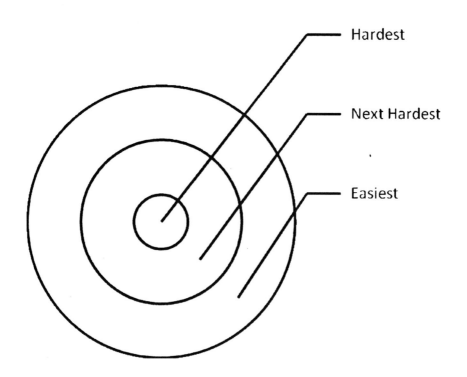

Hardest

Next Hardest

Easiest

FEELING WORDS

Impatience	Envy	Joy
Anger	Frustration	Irritation
Helplessness	Pride	Loneliness
Pain	Anxiety/Worry	Grief
Loss	Paranoia	Hurt
Weakness	Depression	Hopelessness
Love	Guilt	Meanness
Fear	Greed	Jealousy
Doubt	Stubbornness	Content
Superiority	Rebellion	Hope
Selfishness	Sadness	Superiority
Inferiority	Failure	Embarrassment
Rejection	Shame	Disappointment
Satisfaction	Happiness	Power/Control

A Tough Nut to Crack

Family members may be unaware of their strengths. This activity encourages each person to discover the good that lies inside him or her.

1. Therapist shows the family a geode (rocky side first) or picture of a geode and asks if they know what it is.
2. Therapist suggests that the geode is a bit rough on the outside, and rocky looking, but that it holds something very beautiful inside.
3. Therapist then shows the crystalline side of the geode.
4. Therapist reminds family that if someone only looked at the outside of a geode, he or she would miss the best part.
5. Therapist asks family members to share how each of them is like the geode.
6. Therapist asks family members to draw or build a set of family geodes.
7. Each family member makes and decorates a geode using a large plastic egg. The inner crystals may be fashioned from sparkly beads and glitter that are glued inside the egg. Outside, after being coated in craft glue, the egg may be rolled in sand, gravel, or oatmeal to create a rocky exterior.
8. On a separate piece of paper, therapist asks that each family member list the "good things" that are inside his/her geode, waiting to be discovered.
9. Each family member then lists the hard, rocky outer parts of himself/herself that keep others from seeing the remarkable things inside.
10. Family members are invited to add to one another's lists.

Take-It-Home Discussion Questions

Therapist may assign one or more of the following questions for the child to answer and discuss with parent, foster parent, or staff or prior to the next session.

How am I like Polly?
What kinds of "bad" things make someone want to cover up?
Did anything bad happen to me when I was young that I have trouble forgetting?
What do I need to do to be more free and spontaneous in my life?
What is my armor? What do I need to do to take it off?
What sides of me do I hide from others?
Who would I pick to help me take off my armor?

Appendix

Squiggles Stories

This expressive intervention helps assess a child's view of self, others, and the world. It combines an expressive art activity with the concept of mutual storytelling as created by child psychiatrist Richard Alan Gardner in the 1970s. It is an excellent play therapy activity for children and young teens. Children's stories change over time as their perceptions and feelings change. The *Thyme to Heal* and *Bear of a Different Color* stories were created based on squiggles story sessions using the dry erase board.

1. Therapist closes eyes, draws a simple "squiggle" on the dry erase board, opens his or her eyes, and offers a set of markers to the child. (Paper may be used, but we have found that the process is more powerful using the dry erase board. Therapist can photograph the child's artwork to preserve it.)
2. Therapist asks child to complete a drawing from the squiggle.
3. Therapist asks child to tell a short story about his or her drawing—not a story he/she has heard or read, but one he/she makes up.
4. While child tells the story, therapist listens for themes about self, others, and the world.
5. Therapist takes one or more digital photos of the child's drawing, capturing the process and finished product.
6. Therapist asks child to close eyes and make squiggle.
7. Therapist finishes drawing and tells story about it. Therapist parallels child's themes/issues and slightly changes the action and/or outcome to add a problem-solving component, suggestion for change, or positive/realistic twist. Therapist's character can talk out loud and

state some of the main issues that were present in the child's drawing and story.

8. Go back and forth several times. Over the course of treatment, there will be changes in the child's drawing and themes that parallel the child's functioning and views of self, others, and the world.

References

Aposhyan, S. 2005. *Body-mind psychotherapy: Principles, techniques, and practical applications.* New York: Norton.

Bavolek, S. *Nurturing parenting program.* Asheville, NC: Family Development Resources. www.nurturingparents.com.

Brown, P. 1991. *The hypnotic brain: Hypnotherapy and social communication.* New Haven, CT: Yale University Press.

Burns, D. 1980. *Feeling good: The new mood therapy.* New York: HarperCollins.

Burns, G. 2007. *Healing with stories: Your casebook collection for using therapeutic metaphors.* New York: Wiley.

———. 2005. *101 healing stories for kids and teens: Using metaphor in therapy.* New York: Wiley.

Close, H. T. 1998. *Metaphor in psychotherapy: clinical applications of stories and allegories.* Atascadero, CA: Impact Publishers.

Cohen, J., A. E. Deblinger, and A. P. Mannarino. 2004. Trauma-focused cognitive behavioral therapy for sexually abused children. *Psychiatric Times* 21:52–53.

Dozier, M. *Infant Caregiver Project.* University of Delaware, accessed January 11, 2009.

Drewes, A., ed. 2009. *Blending play therapy with cognitive behavioral therapy: Evidence-based and other effective treatments and techniques.* New York: Wiley.

Elliott, D., and J. Briere. 1995. Posttraumatic stress associated with delayed recall of sexual abuse: A general population study. *Journal of Traumatic Stress* 84:629–47.

Fleming, D. C., B. Ritchie, and E. R. Fleming. 1983. Fostering the social adjustment of disturbed students. *Teaching Exceptional Children* 15:172–75.

Gafner, G., and S. Benson. 2003. *Hypnotic techniques: For standard psychotherapy and formal hypnosis.* New York: Norton.

Gil, E., and J. Briere. 2006. *Helping abused and traumatized children: Integrating directive and nondirective approaches.* New York: The Guilford Press.

Greene, R. 2001. *The explosive child: Understanding and helping easily frustrated, "chronically inflexible" children.* New York: HarperCollins.

Harris, H. N., and D. P. Valentiner. 2002. World assumptions, sexual assault, depression, and fearful attitudes toward relationships. *Journal of Interpersonal Violence* 17:286–305.

Hayes, S., V. Follette, and M. Linehan. 2004. *Mindfulness and acceptance: Expanding the cognitive-behavioral tradition.* New York: The Guilford Press.

Hutman, S., J. Jaffe, G. Kemp, J. Saisan, and J. Segal. *Attachment disorders, insecure attachment and reactive attachment disorder*, Joelle Belmonte, www.helpguide.org, accessed January 11, 2009.

Kaduson, H. G., and C. E. Schaeffer, eds. 2003. *101 favorite play therapy techniques, vol. III.* North Vale, NJ: Jason Aronson.

Kinniburgh, K., and M. Blaustein. 2005. Attachment, self-regulation and competency arc outcome trial. *The Trauma Center.* www.traumacenter.org/research/ascot.php, accessed January 11, 2009.

Kinniburgh, K., M. Blaustein, J. Spinnazzola, and B. van der Kolk. 2005. Attachment, self-regulation and competency. *Psychiatric Annals* 35:424–30.

Kopp, R. 1995. *Metaphor therapy: Using client generated metaphors in psychotherapy.* Bristol, PA: Brunner-Mazel.

LeGuin, U. 1968. *A wizard of earthsea.* New York: Bantam Dell.

Levine, P., and A. Frederick. 1997. *Walking the tiger: Healing trauma.* Berkeley, CA: North Atlantic Books.

Mannarino, A. P. 2009. *Empirically supported treatments for childhood trauma: Commonalities and contrasts.* Toronto: American Psychological Association.

McCollum, D. 2006. Child maltreatment and brain development. *Minnesota Medicine* 89(3):48–50. Available online at http://www.minnesotamedicine.com/PastIssues, accessed January 11, 2009.

Morelock, M. J., P. M. Brown, and A. Morrissey. 2003. Pretend play and maternal scaffolding: Comparisons of toddlers with advanced development, typical development, and hearing impairment, *Roeper Review* 26(1):41–51.

O'Hanlon, W., and M. Martin. 1992. *Solution-oriented hypnosis: An Ericksonian approach.* New York: Norton.

Olness, K., and D. Kohen. 1996. *Hypnosis and hypnotherapy with children.* New York: The Guilford Press.

Perry, B. 2008. Attunement: Reading the rhythms of the child. *4Parents Newsletter* (March). http://teacher.scholastic.com/professional/bruceperry/attunement.htm, accessed January 11, 2009.

Prochaska, J. O., and W. F. Velicer. 1997. The transtheoretical model of health behavior change. *American Journal of Health Promotion* 12:38–48.

Robin, A., M. Schneider, and M. Dolnick. 1976. The turtle technique: An extended case study of self-control in the classroom. *Psychology in the Schools* 13:449–53.

Schneider, M. 1974. Turtle technique in the classroom. *Teaching Exceptional Children* 7:21–24.

Schore, A. 1994. *Affect regulation and the origins of the self: The neurobiology of emotional development.* Hillsdale, NJ: Lawrence Erlbaum.

Segal, J., ed. N.d. www.jeannesegal.com/eq/relationships_brain_evolution.html, accessed January 11, 2009.

Siegel, D. 1999. *The developing mind: How relationships and the brain interact to shape who we are.* New York: The Guilford Press.

Smalley, G., and J. Trent. 1993. *The gift of the blessing.* Nashville: Thomas Nelson.

Smith, C., and D. Nylund. 1997. *Narrative therapies with children and adolescents.* New York: The Guilford Press.

Trauma-focused cognitive behavioral therapy. Medical University of South Carolina. www.musc.edu/tfcbt.

van der Kolk, B. 2004. Presentation at the Evolution of Psychotherapy Conference, Anaheim, CA.

Zeig, J. 2008. Workshop: "The utilization of Ericksonian methods in couples and family therapy." Louisville, KY: ZeigTucker.

Index

About the Author

Pat Pernicano, 1985 graduate of Baylor University and licensed clinical psychologist, is director of clinical services at Providence Self Sufficiency Ministries in Georgetown, Indiana. Dr. Pernicano is on the clinical faculty of Spalding University and has worked in the areas of community mental health and residential treatment. She has professional interests in child development, trauma intervention, attachment disruption, child/family therapies (including play therapy), hypnosis, and child assessment. She is grateful to Drs. Jeffrey Zeig, Michael Yapko, Bill O'Hanlon, and Richard Gardner for leading her down the pathways of therapeutic metaphor.

Breinigsville, PA USA
27 August 2010
244402BV00003B/2/P